Soups

Soups

Jane Price

MURDOCH BOOKS

contents

soup kitchen   7

classic   8

hot   46

creamy   86

spicy   120

hearty   158

index   196

soup kitchen

Someone once said 'Soup is cuisine's kindest course'. Soup soothes us when we're ill, feeds us when we're short on time (or money!), curtain-raises at our dinner parties, and provides the best use possible for almost any seasonal produce.

Soup spans seasons, continents, and the whole gamut of ingredients and cooking skills. Soups can be hot or chilled and can even take us travelling to exotic places; to Vietnam, Tunisia, Thailand, or Spain. It is suited to any occasion and comes in a mind-boggling number of colors, consistencies and textures. It can be as familiar a friend as a creamy pumpkin purée, a thick clam chowder, or cheesy French onion soup—menu stalwarts that are never out of vogue.

A soup can have the suave sophistication of classic crab bisque, or be as down-home rustic as pasta and bean or pea and ham. These may be fashioned from humble everyday staples but they're the soups we arguably most love to cook and eat.

Soup loves an accompaniment or two (rolls, dumplings, toast, or croutons) but is equally happy served solo. In fact, the only thing that soup really isn't capable of doing is making itself. Lucky for you, the eager soup cooks of the world, here are all your favorite soup recipes in one indispensable volume.

classic

French onion soup

1¾ oz butter
4 cups finely sliced onions
2 garlic cloves, finely chopped
⅓ cup all-purpose flour
8 cups beef or chicken stock
1 cup dry white wine
1 bay leaf
2 thyme sprigs
12 slices stale baguette
¾ cup finely grated gruyère cheese

Melt the butter in a heavy-based saucepan and add the onion. Cook over low heat, stirring occasionally, for 25 minutes, or until the onion is deep golden brown and beginning to caramelize.

Add the garlic and flour and stir continuously for 2 minutes. Gradually blend in the stock and the wine, stirring continuously, and bring to a boil. Add the bay leaf and thyme and season. Cover the pan and simmer for 25 minutes. Remove the bay leaf and thyme. Preheat the broiler.

Toast the baguette slices, then divide among six soup bowls. Ladle the soup over the top and sprinkle with the grated cheese. Broil until the cheese melts and turns light golden brown. Serve immediately.

SERVES 6

Lentil and Swiss chard soup

Chicken stock
2 lbs 8 oz chicken trimmings
    (neck, ribs, wings), fat
    removed
1 small onion, roughly chopped
1 bay leaf
3–4 Italian parsley sprigs
1–2 oregano or thyme sprigs

1½ cups brown lentils
8 medium Swiss chard stalks
3 tablespoons olive oil
1 large onion, finely chopped
4 garlic cloves, crushed
½ cup finely chopped cilantro
    leaves
4 tablespoons lemon juice
lemon wedges, to serve

To make the stock, put all the ingredients in a large saucepan. Add 12 cups water and bring to a boil. Skim any scum from the surface. Reduce the heat and simmer for 2 hours. Strain the stock, discarding the trimmings, onion, and herbs. Chill overnight. You will need about 4 cups.

Skim any fat from the stock. Put the lentils in a large saucepan, add the stock and 4 cups water. Bring to a boil, then reduce the heat and simmer, covered, for 1 hour.

Meanwhile, remove the stalks from the Swiss chard and shred the leaves. Heat the oil in a saucepan over medium heat and cook the onion for 2–3 minutes, or until transparent. Add the garlic and cook for 1 minute. Add the Swiss chard and toss for 2–3 minutes, or until wilted. Stir the mixture into the lentils. Add the cilantro and lemon juice, season and simmer, covered, for 15–20 minutes. Serve with lemon wedges.

SERVES 6

Pumpkin soup

2 cups vegetable stock
¾ small pumpkin, such as butternut, cut into ½-inch cubes
2 onions, chopped
2 garlic cloves, halved
3 tablespoons light whipping cream
¼ teaspoon ground nutmeg

Put the stock and 2 cups water in a large heavy-based saucepan and bring to a boil. Add the pumpkin, onion, and garlic and return to a boil. Reduce the heat slightly and cook for 15 minutes, or until the pumpkin is soft.

Drain the vegetables in a colander, reserving the liquid. Cool the pumpkin mixture slightly, then purée in a blender until smooth (you may need to add some of the reserved liquid). Return the pumpkin purée to the pan and stir in enough of the reserved liquid to reach the desired consistency.

Serve with cream swirled on top and season to taste with nutmeg, salt and pepper.

SERVES 4

Spring vegetable
soup with basil pesto

5 cups vegetable or chicken stock
1 tablespoon extra virgin olive oil
8 scallions, finely sliced
2 celery stalks, finely sliced
12 baby carrots, sliced
16 thin, fresh asparagus spears, woody ends removed and
    cut into 1¼-inch lengths
¾ cup baby corn, cut into 1¼-inch lengths
¼ cup fresh or bottled pesto
extra virgin olive oil, to thin pesto (see Note)
shaved parmesan cheese, to garnish

Bring the stock to a boil in a large saucepan. Meanwhile, heat the oil in a large heavy-based saucepan and add the scallion and celery. Cover and cook over medium heat for 5 minutes, or until softened.

Add the stock to the scallion mixture and mix well. Add the carrot, asparagus, and corn to the pan. Return the mixture to a boil, then reduce the heat and simmer for 10 minutes.

Top with a dollop of pesto, season to taste, and garnish with shaved parmesan.

SERVES 4

NOTE: Homemade pesto or fresh pesto from a deli will give a better flavor than bottled pesto. If you prefer a thinner pesto, mix it with a little olive oil to give it a runnier consistency.

Crab bisque

1¾ oz butter
½ carrot, finely chopped
½ onion, finely chopped
1 celery stalk, finely
   chopped
1 bay leaf
2 thyme sprigs
2 lbs 4 oz live crabs, cleaned and
   claws detached

2 tablespoons tomato paste
2 tablespoons brandy
⅔ cup dry white wine
4 cups fish stock
⅓ cup rice
3 tablespoons heavy whipping
   cream
¼ teaspoon cayenne pepper

Heat the butter in a large saucepan. Add the vegetables, bay leaf, and thyme and cook over medium heat for 3 minutes, without allowing the vegetables to color. Add the crab claws, legs, and bodies and cook for 5 minutes, or until the crab shells turn red. Add the tomato paste, brandy, and wine and simmer for 2 minutes, or until reduced by half.

Add the stock and 2 cups water and bring to a boil. Reduce the heat and simmer for 5 minutes. Remove the shells, leaving the crab meat in the stock, and reserve the claws to use as a garnish. Finely crush the shells in a mortar and pestle (or in a food processor with a little of the stock).

Return the crushed shells to the soup with the rice. Bring to a boil, reduce the heat, cover and simmer for about 20 minutes, or until the rice is soft.

Immediately strain the bisque into a clean saucepan through a fine sieve lined with damp cheesecloth, pressing down firmly on the solids to extract all the liquid. Add the cream and season with salt and cayenne pepper, then gently reheat. Garnish with the crab claws.

SERVES 4

Spinach soup

1 oz butter
1 onion, finely chopped
3 floury potatoes, grated
4 cups vegetable or chicken stock
1 lb 2 oz frozen chopped spinach
¼ teaspoon ground nutmeg
sour cream, to serve

Melt the butter in a large saucepan over medium heat. Add the onion and cook, stirring occasionally, until soft but not browned.

Add the potato and stock to the pan and mix well, scraping the onion from the bottom of the pan. Add the unthawed spinach and cook, covered, until the spinach has thawed and broken up, stirring occasionally. Uncover and simmer, stirring often, for 10–15 minutes, or until the potato is very soft. Allow to cool slightly, then transfer to a blender or food processor and blend in batches until smooth.

Return the soup to the pan and gently reheat. Add the nutmeg and season. Serve with sour cream swirled on top.

SERVES 4

Chicken and vegetable soup

3 lbs 5 oz chicken
1 onion
2 large leeks, halved lengthways
   and well washed
3 large celery stalks
5 black peppercorns
1 bay leaf
2 large carrots, peeled and
   diced

1 large rutabaga, peeled and
   diced
2 large tomatoes, peeled,
   seeded, and finely chopped
¾ cup barley
1 tablespoon tomato paste
2 tablespoons finely chopped
   Italian parsley

Put the chicken, onion, 1 leek, 1 celery stalk, halved, the peppercorns, and bay leaf in a large saucepan and add enough water to cover. Bring to a boil, then reduce the heat and simmer for 1½ hours, skimming any impurities that rise to the surface.

Strain the stock through a fine sieve and return to the cleaned saucepan. Discard the onion, leek, celery, peppercorns, and bay leaf, and set the chicken aside to cool slightly. Discard the fat and bones, then shred the flesh. Cover with cling wrap and refrigerate.

Allow the stock to cool, then refrigerate overnight. Skim the fat from the surface. Put the stock in a large saucepan and bring to a boil. Dice the remaining leek and celery and add to the soup with the carrot, rutabaga, tomato, barley, and tomato paste. Simmer for 45–50 minutes, or until the vegetables are cooked and the barley is tender. Stir in the parsley and shredded chicken. Simmer until warmed through and season. Serve immediately.

SERVES 4–6

Leek and potato soup

1¾ oz butter
1 onion, finely chopped
3 leeks, white part only, sliced
1 celery stalk, finely chopped
1 garlic clove, finely chopped
2 potatoes, chopped
3 cups chicken stock
¾ cup plus 2 tablespoons light whipping cream
2 tablespoons chopped chives, to garnish

Melt the butter in a large saucepan and add the onion, leek, celery, and garlic. Cover the pan and cook, stirring occasionally, over low heat for 15 minutes, or until the vegetables are softened but not browned. Add the potato and stock and bring to a boil.

Reduce the heat and leave to simmer, covered, for 20 minutes. Allow the soup to cool slightly, then purée in a blender or food processor. Return to the saucepan.

Bring the soup back to a boil and stir in the cream. Season and serve hot or well chilled, garnished with chives.

SERVES 6

Minestrone

½ cup macaroni
1 tablespoon olive oil
1 leek, white part only, sliced
2 garlic cloves, crushed
1 carrot, sliced
1 waxy potato, chopped
1 zucchini, sliced
2 celery stalks, sliced
20 green beans,
    cut into short lengths

1¾ cups canned crushed
    tomatoes
8 cups vegetable or beef stock
2 tablespoons tomato paste
2⅓ cups canned cannellini
    beans, rinsed and drained
2 tablespoons chopped Italian
    parsley
shaved parmesan cheese,
    to serve

Bring a saucepan of water to a boil. Add the macaroni and cook for about 10–12 minutes, or until *al dente*. Drain and return to the pan to keep warm.

Meanwhile, heat the oil in a large heavy-based saucepan. Add the leek and garlic and cook over medium heat for 3–4 minutes.

Add the carrot, potato, zucchini, celery, green beans, tomato, stock, and tomato paste. Bring to a boil, then reduce the heat and simmer for 10 minutes, or until the vegetables are tender.

Stir in the cooked pasta and the cannellini beans and heat through. Garnish with the parsley and shaved parmesan.

SERVES 4

NOTE: Just about any vegetable can be added to minestrone, so this is a great recipe for using up odds and ends.

Caramelized onion and parsnip soup

1 oz butter
3 large onions, halved and thinly sliced
2 tablespoons brown sugar
1 cup dry white wine
3 large parsnips, peeled and chopped
5 cups vegetable stock
3 tablespoons light whipping cream
thyme leaves, to garnish

Melt the butter in a large saucepan. Add the onion and sugar, and cook over low heat for 10 minutes. Add the wine and parsnip, and simmer, covered, for 20 minutes, or until the onion and parsnip are golden and tender.

Pour in the stock, bring to a boil, then reduce the heat and simmer, covered, for 10 minutes. Cool slightly, then place in a blender or food processor and blend in batches until smooth. Season and drizzle with a little cream. Sprinkle the thyme leaves over the top.

SERVES 4

Mushroom soup

1½ oz butter
1 onion, finely chopped
12 large mushrooms, such as portobello, finely chopped
2 garlic cloves, crushed
2 tablespoons dry sherry
4 cups chicken or vegetable stock
heavy whipping cream
2 tablespoons finely chopped Italian parsley

Melt the butter in a large saucepan and fry the onion until the onion is translucent but not brown.

Add the mushroom and garlic and continue frying. The mushrooms might give off a lot of liquid, so fry for 15–20 minutes, or until it is all absorbed back into the mixture.

Add the sherry to the pan, increase the heat and let the mixture bubble—this burns off the alcohol but leaves the flavor. Cool slightly, then transfer to a blender. Process until a smooth paste forms, then add the stock and blend until smooth. Add a couple of tablespoons of cream and blend together. Pour back into the saucepan and heat gently. Garnish with the parsley.

SERVES 4

Gazpacho

8 vine-ripened tomatoes, chopped
1 small cucumber, chopped
1 small red pepper, seeded and chopped
1 red onion, chopped
3 garlic cloves
3 oz sourdough bread, crusts removed
2 tablespoons sherry vinegar
Tabasco sauce

Dressing
2 teaspoons each of finely diced tomato, red pepper,
    red onion, and cucumber
2 teaspoons finely chopped Italian parsley
1 tablespoon extra virgin olive oil
1 teaspoon lemon juice

Combine the tomatoes, cucumber, pepper, onion, garlic, sourdough, and 1 cup cold
water in a blender and blend until smooth. Pass through a strainer into a bowl, and
add the sherry vinegar. Season to taste with salt and Tabasco, then cover and
refrigerate for at least 2 hours, or overnight, to allow the flavors to develop.

To make the dressing, combine all the ingredients in a small bowl. Season.

Stir the gazpacho well. Spoon the dressing over the top before serving.

SERVES 4

Bouillabaisse

Rouille

1 small red pepper

1 slice white bread

1 red chili

2 garlic cloves

1 egg yolk

4 tablespoons olive oil

Soup

2 tablespoons oil

1 onion, chopped

1 medium fennel bulb,
  thinly sliced

6 firm, ripe tomatoes

5 cups fish stock

pinch of saffron threads

bouquet garni

2-inch piece orange zest

3 lbs 5 oz monkfish fillets, cut
  into pieces

18 black mussels, cleaned

To make the rouille, cut the pepper in half, remove the seeds and membrane and place, skin side up, under the broiler until the skin blackens. Cool, then peel away the skin. Chop the pepper flesh. Soak the bread in 3 tablespoons water, then squeeze dry. Put the pepper, bread, chili, garlic, and egg yolk in a food processor and process. Add the oil, mixing until smooth. Cover and refrigerate.

Heat the oil in a large saucepan. Cook the fennel and onion for 5 minutes.

Score a cross in the base of each tomato. Cover with boiling water for 30 seconds, then plunge into cold water. Drain and peel the skin. Chop the tomatoes.

Add the tomato to the saucepan and cook for 3 minutes. Stir in the stock, saffron, bouquet garni, and orange zest, bring to a boil and boil for 10 minutes. Remove the bouquet garni and orange zest and purée in a blender. Return to the pan, season and bring back to a boil. Reduce the heat to a simmer and add the fish and mussels. Cook for 5 minutes, or until the fish is tender and the mussels have opened. Discard any mussels that haven't opened. Serve the soup with the rouille.

SERVES 6

Pea and ham soup

2½ cups yellow or green split peas
1½ tablespoons olive oil
2 onions, chopped
1 carrot, diced
3 celery stalks, finely chopped
2 lbs 4 oz ham bones or smoked hock, chopped
1 bay leaf
2 thyme sprigs
lemon juice, to taste (optional)

Put the split peas in a large bowl, cover with cold water and soak for 6 hours.
Drain well.

Heat the oil in a large saucepan, add the onion, carrot, and celery, and cook over
low heat for 6–7 minutes, or until the vegetables are soft.

Add the split peas, ham bones, bay leaf, thyme, and 10 cups cold water and bring to
a boil. Reduce the heat and simmer, stirring occasionally, for 2 hours, or until the
split peas are tender. Discard the bay leaf and thyme sprigs.

Remove the ham bones from the soup and cool slightly. Remove the meat from the
bone, discard the bones and chop the meat. Return the ham to the soup and reheat.
Season to taste and add lemon juice, if desired.

SERVES 4

Asparagus soup

40 thin, fresh asparagus spears
4 cups vegetable or chicken stock
1 oz butter
1 tablespoon all-purpose flour
½ teaspoon finely grated lemon zest, plus extra, to garnish

Trim and discard any woody ends from the asparagus spears and cut into ¾-inch lengths. Put in a large saucepan and add half the stock. Cover and bring to a boil, then cook for 10 minutes, or until the asparagus is tender. Allow to cool slightly.

Transfer the asparagus mixture to a blender or food processor, and purée in batches until smooth.

Melt the butter in the saucepan over low heat, add the flour, then cook, stirring, for 1 minute, or until pale and foaming. Remove from the heat and gradually add the remaining stock, stirring until smooth after each addition. When all the stock has been added, return the saucepan to the heat, bring to a boil, then simmer for 2 minutes.

Add the asparagus purée to the pan and stir until combined. When heated through, stir in the lemon zest and season. Garnish with the extra lemon zest.

SERVES 4

Borscht

6 large beets, peeled
1½ tablespoons superfine sugar
½ cup lemon juice
3 eggs
sour cream, to serve (optional)

Grate the beets, and put in a saucepan with the sugar and 9 cups water. Stir over low heat until the sugar has dissolved. Simmer, partially covered, for about 30 minutes, skimming the surface occasionally.

Add the lemon juice and simmer, uncovered, for 10 minutes. Remove the pan from the heat.

Whisk the eggs in a bowl. Gradually pour the eggs into the beet mixture, whisking constantly and taking care not to curdle the eggs. Season to taste. Allow the soup to cool, then cover and refrigerate until cold. Served with a dollop of sour cream, if desired.

SERVES 6

Vegetable soup

½ cup dried red kidney beans or cranberry beans
1 tablespoon olive oil
1 leek, white part only, halved lengthways and chopped
1 small onion, diced
2 carrots, chopped
2 celery stalks, chopped
1 large zucchini, chopped
1 tablespoon tomato paste
4 cups vegetable stock
½ small pumpkin, such as butternut, cut into ¾-inch cubes
2 potatoes, cut into ¾-inch cubes
3 tablespoons chopped Italian parsley

Put the beans in a large bowl, cover with cold water and soak overnight. Rinse, then transfer to a saucepan, cover with cold water and cook for 45 minutes, or until just tender. Drain.

Heat the olive oil in a saucepan. Add the leek and onion and cook over medium heat for 2–3 minutes, without browning, or until they start to soften. Add the carrot, celery, and zucchini and cook for 3–4 minutes. Add the tomato paste and stir for 1 minute. Pour in the vegetable stock and 5 cups water and bring to a boil. Reduce the heat to low and simmer for 20 minutes.

Add the pumpkin, potato, parsley, and beans and simmer for a further 20 minutes, or until the vegetables are tender and the beans are cooked. Season well.

SERVES 6

Cabbage soup

½ cup dried navy beans
4½ oz bacon, cubed
1½ oz butter
1 carrot, sliced
1 onion, chopped
1 leek, white part only, roughly chopped
1 turnip, peeled and chopped
bouquet garni
5 cups chicken stock
½ small white cabbage, finely shredded

Soak the beans overnight in cold water. Drain, put in a saucepan and cover with cold water. Bring to a boil and simmer for 5 minutes, then drain. Put the bacon in the same saucepan, cover with water and simmer for 5 minutes. Drain and pat dry with paper towel.

Melt the butter in a large heavy-based saucepan. Add the bacon and cook for 5 minutes, without browning. Add the beans, carrot, onion, leek, and turnip and cook for 5 minutes. Add the bouquet garni and chicken stock and bring to a boil. Cover and simmer for 30 minutes. Add the cabbage, uncover and simmer for 30 minutes, or until the beans are tender. Remove the bouquet garni before serving and season to taste.

SERVES 4

hot

Sweet potato and chili soup

1 tablespoon oil
1 onion, chopped
2 garlic cloves, finely chopped
1–2 small red chillies, finely chopped
¼ teaspoon paprika
5 cups sweet potato,
   chopped into small pieces
4 cups vegetable or beef stock
chopped dried chili, to garnish

Heat the oil in a large heavy-based saucepan. Add the onion and cook for about 1–2 minutes, or until soft. Add the garlic, chili, and paprika and cook for a further 2 minutes, or until aromatic. Add the sweet potato to the pan and toss to coat with the spices.

Pour in the stock and bring to a boil. Reduce the heat and simmer for 15 minutes, or until the vegetables are tender. Cool slightly, then transfer to a blender or food processor and blend in batches until smooth, adding extra water if needed to reach the desired consistency.

Season to taste and sprinkle with dried chili before serving.

SERVES 4

Laksa

5 cups dried rice vermicelli
2 tablespoons peanut oil
2–3 tablespoons laksa paste
4 cups vegetable stock
3 cups coconut milk
3 cups snow peas, halved on the diagonal
5 scallions, cut into 1¼-inch lengths
2 tablespoons lime juice
1½ cups trimmed bean sprouts
7 oz fried tofu puffs, halved
3 tablespoons roughly chopped Vietnamese mint
⅔ cup cilantro leaves

Put the vermicelli in a large bowl, cover with boiling water and soak for 5 minutes.

Heat the oil in a large saucepan, add the laksa paste and cook, stirring, over medium heat for 1 minute, or until fragrant. Add the stock, coconut milk, snow peas, and scallion and simmer for 5 minutes. Pour in the lime juice and season to taste.

Drain the vermicelli and add the bean sprouts and fried tofu puffs. Ladle the hot soup over the vermicelli. Serve immediately, sprinkled with the mint and cilantro.

SERVES 4

Curried chicken noodle soup

2½ cups dried thin egg noodles

2 tablespoons peanut oil

2 boneless, skinless chicken
 breasts (9 oz each)

1 onion, sliced

1 small red chili, seeded and
 finely chopped

1 tablespoon finely chopped
 fresh ginger

2 tablespoons Indian curry
 powder

3 cups chicken stock

3¼ cups coconut milk

10½ oz baby bok choy
 (pak choy), cut into
 long strips

¼ cup torn basil

Cook the noodles in a large saucepan of boiling water for 3–4 minutes, or until soft. Drain well and set aside.

Heat the oil in a large saucepan and add the chicken. Cook on each side for 5 minutes, or until cooked through. Remove the chicken and keep warm.

Put the onion in the pan and cook over low heat for 8 minutes, or until softened but not brown. Add the chili, ginger, and curry powder and cook for a further 2 minutes. Add the chicken stock and bring to a boil. Reduce the heat and simmer for 20 minutes. Thinly slice the chicken on the diagonal.

Add the coconut milk to the saucepan and simmer for 10 minutes. Add the bok choy and cook for 3 minutes, then stir in the basil.

To serve, divide the noodles among four deep serving bowls. Top with slices of chicken and ladle in the soup. Serve immediately.

SERVES 4

Caribbean fish soup

2 firm, ripe tomatoes
2 tablespoons oil
4 shallots, finely chopped
2 celery stalks, chopped
1 large red pepper, chopped
1 Scotch bonnet chili, deseeded
   and finely chopped (see Note)
½ teaspoon ground allspice
½ teaspoon freshly grated
   nutmeg

3½ cups fish stock
2 cups peeled and cubed sweet
   potato
3 tablespoons lime juice
1 lb 2 oz skinless sea bream
   fillets, cut into chunks

Fish substitution
sea bass, cod

Score a cross in the base of each tomato. Soak in boiling water for 30 seconds, then plunge into cold water. Drain and peel the skin away from the cross. Chop the tomatoes, discarding the cores, and reserving any juices.

Heat the oil in a large saucepan, then add the shallots, celery, pepper, chili, allspice, and nutmeg. Cook for 4–5 minutes, or until the vegetables have softened, stirring occasionally. Add the chopped tomatoes (including their juices) and stock and bring to a boil. Reduce the heat to medium and add the sweet potato. Season to taste and cook for about 15 minutes, or until the sweet potato is tender.

Add the lime juice and chunks of fish to the saucepan and poach gently for 4–5 minutes, or until the fish is cooked through. Season to taste.

SERVES 6

NOTE: Scotch bonnet chilies look like a mini pepper and can be green, red, or orange. They are extremely hot but have a good, slightly acidic flavor.

Chicken and galangal soup

2- x ¾-inch piece fresh galangal, peeled and cut into thin slices
2 cups coconut milk
1 cup chicken stock
4 kaffir lime leaves, torn
1 tablespoon finely chopped cilantro roots
1 lb 2 oz boneless, skinless chicken breasts, cut into thin strips
1–2 teaspoons finely chopped red chilies
2 tablespoons fish sauce
1½ tablespoons lime juice
3 teaspoons palm sugar or brown sugar
⅓ cup chopped cilantro leaves

Place the galangal in a saucepan with the coconut milk, stock, kaffir lime leaves, and cilantro roots. Bring to a boil, reduce the heat to low and simmer for 10 minutes, stirring occasionally.

Add the chicken and chili to the pan and simmer for 8 minutes.

Stir in the fish sauce, lime juice, and palm sugar and cook for 1 minute. Stir in the cilantro leaves. Serve immediately garnished with extra cilantro, if desired.

SERVES 4

Beef pho

7 oz rice noodle sticks
6 cups beef stock
1 star anise
1½-inch piece fresh ginger, sliced
2 pig's feet
½ onion, studded with 2 cloves
2 lemon grass stems, white part only, pounded
2 garlic cloves, pounded
¼ teaspoon white pepper
1 tablespoon fish sauce
14 oz beef fillet, partially frozen, and thinly sliced
1 cup trimmed bean sprouts

2 scallions, thinly sliced on the diagonal
½ cup chopped cilantro leaves
½ cup chopped Vietnamese mint
1 red chili, thinly sliced, plus extra, to serve
Vietnamese mint, extra, to serve
cilantro leaves, extra, to serve
2 limes, cut into quarters
fish sauce, extra, to serve

Soak the noodles in boiling water for 15–20 minutes. Drain.

Bring the stock, star anise, ginger, pig's feet, onion, lemon grass, garlic, and white pepper to a boil in a large saucepan. Reduce the heat and simmer for 30 minutes. Strain, return to the same pan and stir in the fish sauce.

Divide the noodles among bowls, then top with beef strips, bean sprouts, scallion, cilantro, mint, and chili. Ladle on the broth.

Put the extra chili, mint, cilantro, lime quarters, and fish sauce in small bowls on a platter and serve with the soup.

SERVES 4

Mexican soup with salsa

3 tablespoons olive oil
1 large onion, chopped
1 large celery stalk, chopped
3 garlic cloves, crushed
2 thin red chilies, chopped
3 cups fish stock, plus
   1 tablespoon extra
3½ cups canned crushed
   tomatoes
2 bay leaves
1 teaspoon dried oregano
1 teaspoon superfine sugar
2 medium ears of corn, kernels
   removed
1 lb 2 oz halibut fillets

2 tablespoons chopped cilantro
   leaves
juice of 2 limes
12 shrimp, tails intact
8 scallops, cleaned
12 clams, cleaned
½ cup heavy whipping cream

Salsa
½ small avocado
1 tablespoon cilantro leaves
grated zest and juice of 1 lime
½ red onion, finely chopped

Heat the oil in a saucepan. Add the onion and celery and cook over medium heat for 10 minutes. Add the garlic and chili and cook for 1 minute, stirring. Add the fish stock and tomatoes. Stir in the bay leaves, oregano, and sugar and bring to a boil. Reduce the heat to low and simmer for 10 minutes. Remove the bay leaves, then tip the slightly cooled tomato mixture into a food processor and whiz until smooth. Return the tomato sauce to the pan and season. Add the corn kernels and bring back to a boil. Reduce the heat and simmer for 3 minutes. Cut the fish into chunks. Stir the cilantro and the lime juice into the sauce, add the fish, then simmer for 1 minute. Add the shrimp, scallops, and clams. Cover with a lid and cook for a further 2–3 minutes, or until the seafood is cooked through.

To make the salsa, chop the avocado into cubes and mix with the cilantro, the lime zest and juice, and red onion. Stir the cream into the soup and top with salsa.

SERVES 4

Thai spicy sour soup

3 cups vegetable stock
2 tablespoons tom yum paste (see Note)
¾- x ¾-inch piece galangal,
    peeled and cut into thin slices
1 lemon grass stem, white part only, lightly crushed and cut into 4
    lengths
3 kaffir lime leaves
1 small red chili, finely sliced on the diagonal (optional)
3 cups halved button mushrooms
¾ cup cubed silken firm tofu
7 oz baby bok choy (pak choy), roughly shredded
2 tablespoons lime juice
1 small handful cilantro leaves

Place the stock, tom yum paste, galangal, lemon grass, kaffir lime leaves, chili, and 3 cups water in a saucepan. Cover and bring to a boil, then reduce the heat and simmer for 5 minutes.

Add the mushrooms and tofu and simmer for 5 minutes, or until the mushrooms are tender. Add the bok choy and simmer for a further minute, or until wilted. Remove the pan from the heat and stir in the lime juice and cilantro leaves before serving.

SERVES 4–6

NOTE: For vegetarian cooking, make sure you buy a brand of tom yum paste that does not contain shrimp paste or fish sauce.

Chicken and pumpkin laksa

Paste

2 bird's eye chilies, chopped
2 lemon grass stems, white part only, chopped
4 shallots, peeled
1 tablespoon chopped fresh ginger
1 teaspoon ground turmeric
3 roasted candlenuts (optional)

3¾ oz dried rice noodle sticks
1 tablespoon peanut oil
¼ small pumpkin, such as butternut, cut into chunks

3¼ cups coconut milk
1 lb 5 oz boneless, skinless chicken breasts, cut into cubes
2 tablespoons lime juice
1 tablespoon fish sauce
1 cup bean sprouts
½ cup torn basil
½ cup torn mint
½ cup unsalted peanuts, toasted and chopped
1 lime, cut into quarters

Put all the paste ingredients in a food processor with 1 tablespoon of water and blend until smooth.

Soak the noodles in boiling water for 15–20 minutes. Drain.

Meanwhile, heat the oil in a wok and swirl to coat. Add the paste and stir over low heat for 5 minutes, or until aromatic. Add the squash and coconut milk and simmer for 10 minutes. Add the chicken and simmer for 20 minutes. Stir in the lime juice and fish sauce.

Divide the noodles among four deep serving bowls, then ladle the soup over them. Top with the bean sprouts, basil, mint, peanuts, and lime.

SERVES 4

Curried lentil, carrot, and cashew soup

6 cups vegetable or chicken stock
6 carrots, grated
¾ cup red lentils, rinsed and drained
1 tablespoon olive oil
1 large onion, chopped
½ cup unsalted cashew nuts
1 tablespoon Madras curry paste
½ cup chopped cilantro leaves and stems
½ cup Greek-style yogurt
cilantro leaves, to garnish

Bring the stock to a boil in a large saucepan. Add the carrot and lentils, bring the mixture back to a boil. Simmer over low heat for about 8 minutes, or until the carrot and lentils are soft.

Meanwhile, heat the oil in a large frying pan. Add the onion and cashews and cook over medium heat for 2–3 minutes, or until the onion is soft and browned. Add the curry paste and cilantro and cook for a further 1 minute, or until fragrant. Stir the paste into the carrot and lentil mixture. Allow to cool slightly.

Transfer to a food processor or blender and process in batches until smooth. Return the mixture to the pan and reheat over medium heat until hot. Season to taste and serve with a dollop of yogurt and a sprinkling of cilantro.

SERVES 6

NOTE: Garnish the soup with a pinch of chilli flakes to give it an extra kick.

Vietnamese beef soup

14 oz rump steak, trimmed
½ onion
1½ tablespoons fish sauce
1 star anise
1 cinnamon stick
pinch ground white pepper
6 cups beef stock
10½ oz fresh, thin rice noodles
3 scallions, thinly sliced
¾ cup Vietnamese mint leaves
1 cup trimmed bean sprouts

1 small white onion, cut in half
   and thinly sliced
1 small red chili, thinly sliced
   on the diagonal
lemon wedges, to serve

Wrap the rump steak in cling wrap and freeze for 40 minutes.

Meanwhile, put the onion, fish sauce, star anise, cinnamon stick, pepper, stock, and 2 cups water in a large saucepan. Bring to a boil, then reduce the heat, cover and simmer for 20 minutes. Discard the onion, star anise, and cinnamon stick.

Cover the noodles with boiling water and gently separate the strands. Drain and refresh under cold water.

Remove the meat from the freezer and thinly slice it across the grain.

Divide the noodles and scallion among four deep bowls. Top with the beef, mint, bean sprouts, onion, and chili. Ladle the hot broth over the top and serve with the lemon wedges.

SERVES 4

NOTE: In Vietnam, noodle soups are called pho — beef noodle soup, pho bo, is one of the most popular.

Pumpkin and red lentil soup

1 tablespoon olive oil
1 long red chili, seeded and chopped
1 onion, finely chopped
½ small pumpkin, such as butternut, chopped
2½ cups chopped sweet potato
6 cups vegetable stock
½ cup red lentils
1 tablespoon tahini
red chili, extra, to garnish

Heat the oil in a large saucepan over medium heat. Add the chili and onion and cook for 2–3 minutes, or until the onion is soft. Reduce the heat to low, add the pumpkin and sweet potato and cook, covered, for 8 minutes, stirring occasionally.

Increase the heat to high, add the stock and bring to a boil. Reduce the heat to low, and simmer, covered, for 10 minutes. Add the red lentils and cook, covered, for 7 minutes, or until tender.

Process the soup in batches in a blender or food processor. Add the tahini and blend until smooth. Return to the saucepan and gently heat until warmed through. Garnish with chili.

SERVES 4

Rice noodle soup with duck

1 whole Chinese roast duck
4 cilantro roots and stems, well
  rinsed
5 slices fresh galangal
4 scallions, sliced on the
  diagonal into 1¼-inch
  lengths
14 oz Chinese broccoli (gai larn),
  cut into 2-inch lengths
2 garlic cloves, crushed
3 tablespoons fish sauce

1 tablespoon hoisin sauce
2 teaspoons grated palm sugar
  or brown sugar
½ teaspoon ground white
  pepper
1 lb 2 oz fresh rice noodles
crispy fried garlic flakes,
  to garnish (optional)
cilantro leaves,
  to garnish (optional)

To make the stock, cut off the duck's head and discard. Remove the skin and fat, leaving the neck intact. Remove the flesh from the bones and set aside. Cut any fat from the carcass along with the parson's nose, then discard. Break the carcass into pieces, then put in a stockpot with 8 cups water.

Bruise the cilantro roots and stems with the back of a knife. Add to the pot with the galangal and bring to a boil. Skim off any foam from the surface. Boil over medium heat for 15 minutes. Strain the stock through a fine sieve, discard the carcass, and return the stock to a clean saucepan.

Slice the duck flesh into strips. Add to the stock with the scallion, Chinese broccoli, garlic, fish sauce, hoisin sauce, palm sugar, and white pepper. Gently bring to a boil.

Cook the noodles in boiling water for 2–3 minutes, or until tender. Drain well. Divide the noodles and soup evenly among the serving bowls. If desired, garnish with the garlic flakes and cilantro leaves.

SERVES 4–6

Hot and sour
shrimp soup

12 oz raw medium shrimp
1 tablespoon oil
3 lemon grass stems, white part only
3 thin slices fresh galangal
3–5 small red chilies
5 kaffir lime leaves, finely shredded
2 tablespoons fish sauce
2 scallions, sliced

½ cup canned straw mushrooms, drained, or quartered button mushrooms
3 tablespoons lime juice
1–2 tablespoons chili paste, or to taste
cilantro leaves, to garnish (optional)

Peel and devein the shrimp, leaving the tails intact and reserving the heads and shells.

Heat the oil in a large stockpot or wok and add the shrimp heads and shells. Cook for 5 minutes, or until the shells turn bright orange. Bruise 1 stem of the lemon grass with the back of a knife. Add to the pan with the galangal and 8 cups water. Bring to a boil, then reduce the heat and simmer for 20 minutes. Strain the stock and return to the pan. Discard the shells, lemon grass, and galangal.

Finely slice the chilies and remaining lemon grass. Add to the liquid with the kaffir lime leaves, fish sauce, scallion, and mushrooms. Cook gently for 2 minutes.

Add the shrimp and cook for 3 minutes, or until the shrimp are tender. Add the lime juice and chili paste (adjust to taste with extra lime juice or fish sauce). If desired, garnish with cilantro leaves.

SERVES 4–6

Green curry
vegetable soup

2 teaspoons peanut oil
1 tablespoon green curry paste
3 kaffir lime leaves
5 cups vegetable or chicken stock
2⅔ cups coconut milk
½ small winter squash, such as butternut,
    cut into ½-inch cubes
9 oz small yellow (pattypan) squash, sliced
⅔ cup fresh baby corn spears, halved lengthways
2 tablespoons mushroom soy sauce
2 tablespoons lime juice
1 teaspoon sugar
1½ tablespoons finely chopped Vietnamese mint

Heat the oil in a large saucepan and add the curry paste and kaffir lime leaves. Cook, stirring, over medium heat for 1 minute, or until fragrant.

Bring the stock to the boil in a separate saucepan.

Gradually add the stock and coconut milk to the curry mixture and bring to a boil. Add the squash, small yellow squash, and corn, and simmer over low heat for 12 minutes, or until the butternut squash is tender.

Add the soy sauce and lime juice, and season to taste with sugar, salt, and black pepper. Garnish with the mint before serving.

SERVES 6

Beef and chili bean soup

1 tablespoon oil
1 red onion, finely chopped
2 garlic cloves, crushed
2½ teaspoons chili flakes
2½ teaspoons ground cumin
2½ tablespoons finely chopped cilantro root and stem
1½ teaspoons ground coriander
1 lb 2 oz lean ground beef
1 tablespoon tomato paste
4 firm, ripe tomatoes, peeled, seeded, and diced
2⅓ cups canned red kidney beans, drained and rinsed
8 cups beef stock
3 tablespoons chopped cilantro leaves
⅓ cup sour cream, to serve

Heat the oil in a large saucepan over medium heat. Cook the onion for about 2–3 minutes, or until softened. Add the garlic, chili flakes, cumin, and fresh and ground coriander, and cook for 1 minute. Add the beef and cook for 3–4 minutes, or until cooked through—break up any lumps with a spoon.

Add the tomato paste, tomato, beans, and stock and bring to a boil. Reduce the heat and simmer for 15–20 minutes, or until reduced slightly. Remove any scum on the surface. Stir in the chopped cilantro. Serve with sour cream.

SERVES 4

Gumbo

Roux

4 tablespoons oil

⅔ cup all-purpose flour

1 onion, finely chopped

4 crabs, cleaned

1 lb chorizo sausage, cut into bite-sized pieces

6 scallions, sliced

1 green pepper, roughly chopped

3 tablespoons chopped Italian parsley

¼ teaspoon chili powder

1 lb 2 oz shrimp, peeled and deveined

24 oysters, shucked

½ teaspoon filé powder (see Note)

1½ tablespoons long-grain rice

To make the roux, pour the oil into a heavy-based saucepan over low heat. Add the flour, stirring after each addition, to make a thin roux. Continue to stir over low heat for 35 minutes, or until dark brown. Add the onion and cook for 4 minutes, or until tender. Pour in 6 cups boiling water, stirring to dissolve the roux, and bring to a simmer.

Cut the crabs into pieces. Add the crab, sausage, scallion, pepper, parsley, and chili powder to the roux. Cook for 30 minutes, then add the shrimp and the oysters and their juices and cook for a further 5 minutes, or until the shrimp are pink. Season well, then stir in the filé powder.

Meanwhile, cook the rice in boiling salted water for about 10 minutes, or until just cooked through. Put a couple of tablespoons of rice in the bottom of each bowl and ladle over the gumbo. Serve immediately.

SERVES 6

NOTE: Filé powder is a flavoring often used in Creole cooking. It is made by drying, then grinding sassafras leaves.

Tom yum goong

1 tablespoon oil
1 lb 2 oz shrimp, peeled and
    deveined, reserving the heads
    and shells
2 tablespoons Thai red curry
    paste or tom yum paste
2 tablespoons tamarind purée
    (see Note)
2 teaspoons ground turmeric
1 teaspoon chopped red chilies

4 kaffir lime leaves, shredded
2 tablespoons fish sauce
2 tablespoons lime juice
2 teaspoons grated palm sugar
    or brown sugar
2 tablespoons cilantro leaves

Heat the oil in a large saucepan or wok and cook the shrimp heads and shells for
10 minutes over medium heat, stirring frequently, until the heads are deep orange
in color.

Add 1 cup water and the curry paste to the saucepan. Bring to a boil and cook for 5
minutes, or until reduced slightly. Add another 8 cups water and simmer for 20
minutes. Strain, discarding the shells and heads, and pour the stock back into
the pan.

Add the tamarind, turmeric, chilies, and kaffir lime leaves to the saucepan. Bring to a
boil and cook for 2 minutes. Add the shrimp and cook for 5 minutes, or until pink.
Stir in the fish sauce, lime juice, and sugar. Serve sprinkled with cilantro leaves.

SERVES 4–6

NOTE: If you are unable to find tamarind purée, you can make your own by
soaking an 8-ounce packet of tamarind pulp in 2 cups boiling water for 1–2 hours,
crushing occasionally. Push through a sieve and discard the fibers. Alternatively, use
lemon juice.

Chili, corn, and red pepper soup

1 cilantro sprig
4 sweet ears of corn
1 oz butter
2 red peppers, diced
1 small onion, finely chopped
1 small red chili, finely chopped
1 tablespoon all-purpose flour
2 cups vegetable stock
½ cup light whipping cream

Trim the leaves off the cilantro and finely chop the root and stems. Cut the kernels off the ears of corn.

Heat the butter in a saucepan over medium heat. Add the corn kernels, pepper, onion, and chili and stir to coat in the butter. Cook, covered, over low heat, stirring occasionally, for 10 minutes, or until soft. Increase the heat to medium, add the cilantro root and stem and cook, stirring, for 30 seconds, or until fragrant. Sprinkle with the flour and stir for 1 minute. Remove from the heat and gradually stir in the stock. Add 2 cups water and return to the heat. Bring to a boil, reduce the heat to low and simmer, covered, for 30 minutes, or until the vegetables are tender. Cool slightly.

Pour 2 cups of the soup into a blender and purée until smooth. Return the purée to the soup in the pan, pour in the cream and gently heat until warmed through. Season. Sprinkle with the cilantro leaves.

SERVES 4

creamy

Zucchini pesto soup

1 tablespoon olive oil
1 large onion, finely chopped
2 garlic cloves, crushed
3 cups vegetable or chicken
   stock
8 zucchini, thinly sliced
3 tablespoons light whipping
   cream
toasted ciabatta, to serve

Pesto
1 cup basil
¼ cup finely grated parmesan
   cheese
2 tablespoons pine nuts, toasted
2 tablespoons extra virgin
   olive oil

Heat the oil in a large heavy-based saucepan. Add the onion and garlic and cook over medium heat for 5 minutes, or until the onion is soft.

Bring the stock to a boil in a separate saucepan. Add the zucchini and hot stock to the onion mixture. Bring to a boil, then reduce the heat. Cover and simmer for 10 minutes, or until the zucchini is very soft.

To make the pesto, process the basil, parmesan, and pine nuts in a food processor for 20 seconds, or until finely chopped. Gradually add the olive oil and process until smooth. Spoon into a small bowl.

Transfer the zucchini mixture to a blender or food processor and blend in batches until smooth. Return the mixture to the pan, stir in the cream and 2 tablespoons of the pesto, and reheat over medium heat until hot. Season and serve with toasted ciabatta, if desired.

SERVES 4

Orange
sweet potato soup

1½ oz butter
2 onions, chopped
2 garlic cloves, crushed
6⅔ cups peeled and chopped sweet potato
1 large celery stalk, chopped
1 large green apple, peeled, cored, and chopped
1½ teaspoons ground cumin
8 cups chicken stock
½ cup plain yogurt
soft Armenian cracker bread, to serve (optional)

Melt the butter in a large saucepan over low heat. Add the onion and cook, stirring occasionally, for 10 minutes, or until soft. Add the garlic, sweet potato, celery, apple, and 1 teaspoon of the cumin and cook for 5–7 minutes, or until well coated. Add the stock and the remaining cumin and bring to a boil over high heat. Reduce the heat and simmer for 25–30 minutes, or until the sweet potato is very soft.

Cool the soup slightly and blend in batches until smooth. Return to the pan and gently stir over medium heat until warmed through. Season and serve with a dollop of yogurt and toasted cracker bread, if desired.

SERVES 4–6

Shrimp, potato, and corn chowder

1 lb 5 oz raw medium shrimp
3 ears of corn, husks removed
1 tablespoon olive oil
2 leeks, white part only,
    finely chopped
2 garlic cloves, crushed

4 potatoes, cut into ½-inch
    cubes
3 cups fish or chicken stock
1½ cups whole milk
1 cup light whipping cream
pinch cayenne pepper
3 tablespoons finely chopped
    Italian parsley

Peel and devein the shrimp then chop into small pieces. Cut the kernels from the ears of corn.

Heat the oil in a large saucepan and add the leek. Cook over medium–low heat for about 5 minutes, or until soft and lightly golden. Add the garlic and cook for 30 seconds, then add the corn, potato, stock, and milk.

Bring to a boil, then reduce the heat. Simmer, partially covered, for 20 minutes, or until the potato is soft but still holds its shape. Remove the lid and simmer for a further 10 minutes to allow the soup to thicken. Reduce the heat to low. Put 2 cups of the soup in a blender and blend until very smooth.

Return the blended soup to the saucepan and add the shrimp. Increase the heat to medium and simmer for 2 minutes, or until the shrimp are pink and cooked through. Stir in the cream, cayenne pepper, and 2 tablespoons of the parsley. Season to taste, then serve garnished with the remaining parsley.

SERVES 4–6

Fresh mushroom,
shallot, and sour cream soup

1½ oz butter
⅔ cup chopped shallots
3 garlic cloves, crushed
1½ cups Italian parsley
1¼ cups vegetable or chicken stock
1¼ cups whole milk
9 cups chopped button mushrooms,
   plus extra, to garnish (optional)
¼ teaspoon ground nutmeg
¼ teaspoon cayenne pepper, plus extra, to garnish
⅔ cup light sour cream

Melt the butter in a large heavy-based saucepan and add the shallots, garlic, and parsley. Cook over medium heat for 2–3 minutes.

Put the stock and milk in a separate saucepan and bring to a boil.

Add the mushrooms to the shallot mixture. Season, then stir in the nutmeg and cayenne pepper. Cook, stirring, for 1 minute. Add the stock and milk, bring to a boil, then reduce the heat and simmer for 5 minutes. Transfer the soup to a blender or food processor and blend until smooth. Return to the pan.

Stir in the sour cream and reheat gently. Season to taste and serve sprinkled with cayenne pepper. Garnish with the extra mushrooms, lightly fried in butter, if desired.

SERVES 4

Watercress soup

1 oz butter
1 onion, finely chopped
2 potatoes, diced
2½ cups chicken stock
2 lbs 4 oz watercress, trimmed and chopped
½ cup light whipping cream
½ cup whole milk
freshly grated nutmeg
2 tablespoons chopped chives

Melt the butter in a large saucepan and add the onion. Cover the pan and cook over low heat until the onion is softened. Add the potato and chicken stock and simmer for 12 minutes, or until the potato is tender. Add the watercress and cook for 1 minute.

Remove from the heat and leave the soup to cool a little. Pour into a blender or food processor and blend until smooth. Return to the saucepan.

Bring the soup gently back to a boil and stir in the cream and milk. Season with nutmeg, salt, and pepper and reheat without boiling. Serve garnished with chives.

SERVES 4

Creamy chicken and corn soup

3/4 oz butter
1 tablespoon olive oil
1 lb 2 oz boneless, skinless
  chicken thighs,
  thinly sliced
2 garlic cloves, chopped
1 leek, white part only, chopped
1 large celery stalk, chopped
1 bay leaf
1/2 teaspoon thyme

4 cups chicken stock
3 tablespoons sherry
2 3/4 cups corn kernels (fresh,
  canned, or frozen)
1 large floury potato, cut into
  1/2-inch cubes
3/4 cup light whipping cream
chives, to garnish

Melt the butter and oil in a large saucepan over high heat. Cook the chicken in batches for 3 minutes, or until lightly golden and just cooked through. Place in a bowl, cover and refrigerate until needed.

Reduce the heat to medium and stir in the garlic, leek, celery, bay leaf, and thyme. Cook for 2 minutes, or until the leek softens. Add the stock, sherry, and 2 cups water and stir to combine. Add the corn and potato and bring to a boil. Reduce the heat and simmer for 1 hour, skimming any scum off the surface. Cool slightly.

Remove the bay leaf and purée the soup in a blender or food processor. Return to the pan and add the cream and chicken. Stir over medium heat for 2–3 minutes, or until heated through. Season. Serve with extra cream and garnish with chives.

SERVES 4–6

Corn and lemon grass soup with crayfish

4 ears of corn
1 tablespoon oil
1 leek, white part only, chopped
1 celery stalk, chopped
3 lemon grass stems, white part
   only, bruised
5 garlic cloves, crushed
1 teaspoon ground cumin
1 teaspoon ground coriander
¾ teaspoon ground white pepper

3 kaffir lime leaves
3 cups chicken stock
3¼ cups coconut milk
½ cup light whipping cream
2 teaspoons butter
½ teaspoon sambal oelek
2 lbs 10 oz cooked crayfish,
   shredded
1 tablespoon finely chopped
   cilantro leaves

Trim the kernels from the corn. Heat the oil in a saucepan over medium heat. Add the leek, celery, and lemon grass. Stir for 10 minutes, or until the leek is soft. Add half the garlic, the cumin, coriander, and ½ teaspoon of the pepper. Cook, stirring, for 1–2 minutes, or until fragrant. Add the corn, kaffir lime leaves, stock, and coconut milk, stir well and simmer for 1½ hours. Remove from the heat and cool. Remove the lemon grass and kaffir lime leaves and blend the mixture in batches in a food processor.

Push the mixture through a sieve. Repeat. Return to a saucepan, add the cream and warm gently.

Melt the butter in a frying pan over medium heat, add the remaining garlic, sambal oelek, remaining pepper, and a pinch of salt and stir for 1 minute. Add the crayfish meat, stir for a further minute, then remove from the heat and stir in the cilantro. Ladle into bowls, piling the crayfish mixture into the middle.

SERVES 4

Cauliflower and almond soup with hot cheese rolls

½ cup blanched almonds
1 tablespoon olive oil
1 leek, white part only, chopped
2 garlic cloves, crushed
1 small cauliflower, cut into
   small florets
2 all-purpose potatoes, cut into
   ½-inch pieces
7 cups chicken stock

Cheese rolls
4 round bread rolls
1½ oz softened butter
1 cup grated cheddar cheese
⅔ cup grated parmesan cheese

Preheat the oven to 350°F. Put the almonds on a baking tray and toast for 5 minutes, or until golden.

Heat the oil in a large saucepan over medium heat and cook the leek for 2–3 minutes, or until softened. Add the garlic and cook for 30 seconds, then add the cauliflower, potato, and stock. Bring to a boil, then reduce the heat and simmer for 15 minutes, or until the vegetables are very tender. Cool for 5 minutes.

Blend the soup with the almonds in batches in a blender until smooth. Season to taste. Return to the pan and stir over medium heat until heated through. Serve with the cheese rolls, if desired.

To make the cheese rolls, split the rolls and butter both sides. Combine the grated cheeses and divide evenly among the rolls. Sandwich together and wrap in foil. Bake in the oven for 15–20 minutes, or until the cheese has melted.

SERVES 4

Potato and
sweet corn chowder

6 sweet ears of corn
2 tablespoons vegetable oil
1 onion, finely diced
3 garlic cloves, crushed
1 celery stalk, diced
1 carrot, peeled and diced
2 large potatoes, peeled and diced
4 cups vegetable or chicken stock
2 tablespoons finely chopped Italian parsley

Bring a large saucepan of salted water to a boil. Cook the sweet corn for 5 minutes. Reserve 1 cup of the cooking water. Cut the kernels from the ears of corn, place half in a blender with the reserved cooking water, and blend until smooth.

Heat the oil in a large saucepan. Add the onion, garlic, celery, and a large pinch of salt and cook for 5 minutes. Add the carrot and potato, cook for a further 5 minutes, then add the stock, corn kernels, and blended corn mixture. Reduce the heat and simmer for 20 minutes, or until the vegetables are tender. Season well and stir in the chopped parsley before serving.

SERVES 6

Cream of fennel and leek soup

1 oz butter
2 large fennel bulbs, thinly
  sliced
2 leeks, white part only, thinly
  sliced
4 cups hot vegetable or chicken
  stock
2 rosemary sprigs
⅛ teaspoon ground nutmeg
⅓ cup sour cream

¼ cup finely grated parmesan
  cheese
1 tablespoon oil
1 leek, white part only, extra,
  cut in half lengthways, and
  cut into 1½-inch lengths
grated parmesan cheese, extra,
  to garnish
sour cream, extra, to garnish

Heat the butter in a large heavy-based saucepan and add the sliced fennel and leek. Cook, covered, over medium heat for 2–3 minutes, stirring occasionally.

Put the hot stock, rosemary sprigs, and nutmeg in a saucepan and bring to a boil. Simmer over low heat for about 15 minutes, then remove the rosemary sprigs and add the fennel and leek mixture to the pan.

Transfer the soup to a blender or food processor and blend in batches until smooth. Return to the pan and stir in the sour cream and parmesan. Reheat over medium heat until hot. Season to taste and keep warm.

Heat the oil in a frying pan and cook the extra leek for 2–3 minutes, or until soft but not browned.

Top the soup with the fried leek and garnish with the extra parmesan and sour cream. Serve immediately.

SERVES 6

Chicken, mushroom, and Madeira soup

½ cup dried porcini mushrooms
1 oz butter
1 leek, white part only,
    thinly sliced
9 oz pancetta, chopped
3 cups roughly chopped brown
    mushrooms
2 large mushrooms, such as
    portobello, chopped
2 tablespoons all-purpose flour
½ cup dry Madeira
5 cups chicken stock

1 tablespoon olive oil
2 boneless, skinless chicken
    breasts (about 7 oz each)
⅓ cup light sour cream
2 teaspoons chopped marjoram,
    plus whole leaves, to garnish

Soak the porcini in 1 cup of boiling water for 20 minutes.

Melt the butter in a large saucepan over medium heat and add the leek and pancetta. Cook for 5 minutes, or until the leek is softened. Add all the mushrooms and the porcini soaking liquid and cook for 10 minutes. Stir in the flour and cook for 1 minute. Add the Madeira and cook, stirring, for 10 minutes. Stir in the stock, bring to a boil, then reduce the heat and simmer for 45 minutes. Cool slightly.

Heat the oil in a frying pan and cook the chicken for 4–5 minutes each side, or until cooked through. Remove from the pan and thinly slice.

Blend the soup until smooth. Return to the saucepan, add the sour cream and chopped marjoram and stir over medium heat for about 1–2 minutes to warm through. Season. Top with the chicken and garnish with marjoram.

SERVES 4

Creamy clam soup

4 lbs clams, cleaned
1¾ oz butter
1 onion, chopped
1 celery stalk, chopped
1 large carrot, chopped
1 large leek, white part only,
   sliced into rings
2 cups diced rutabaga
3¼–4 cups fish stock
1 bay leaf

⅓ cup medium- or short-grain
   rice
¾ cup light whipping cream,
   plus 1 tablespooon extra
3 tablespoons finely chopped
   Italian parsley

Put the clams and 1 cup water in a large saucepan. Bring to a boil, then reduce the heat to medium and cover with a tight-fitting lid. Cook for 3–4 minutes, or until the shells open. Strain into a bowl. Add enough stock to make up to 4 cups. Discard any clams that haven't opened. Remove all but eight of the clams from their shells.

Melt the butter in a saucepan. Add the vegetables and cook, covered, over medium heat for 10 minutes, stirring occasionally. Add the stock and bay leaf, bring to a boil, then reduce the heat and simmer for 10 minutes. Add the rice, bring back to a boil, cover and cook over medium heat for 15 minutes, or until the rice and vegetables are tender. Remove from the heat and stir in the clam meat. Remove the bay leaf and allow to cool for 10 minutes.

Purée the soup in a blender until smooth, then return to a saucepan. Stir in the cream and season. Gently reheat the soup. Add the parsley and two clams in the shell to each bowl.

SERVES 4

Sweet potato and pear soup

1 oz butter
1 small white onion, finely chopped
5 cups peeled and cubed sweet potato
2 firm medium pears, peeled, cored, and
    cut into ¾-inch cubes
3 cups vegetable or chicken stock
1 cup light whipping cream
mint leaves, to garnish

Melt the butter in a saucepan over medium heat. Add the onion and cook for 2–3 minutes, or until softened. Add the sweet potato and pear, and cook, stirring, for 1–2 minutes. Add the stock, bring to a boil and cook for 20 minutes, or until the sweet potato and pear are soft.

Cool slightly, then place the mixture in a blender or food processor and blend in batches until smooth. Return to the pan, stir in the cream and gently reheat without boiling. Season and garnish with the mint.

SERVES 4

New England
clam chowder

3 lbs 5 oz clams, cleaned
2 teaspoons oil
3 bacon slices, chopped
1 onion, chopped
1 garlic clove, crushed
5 potatoes, diced

1⅓ cups fish stock
2 cups whole milk
½ cup light whipping cream
3 tablespoons chopped
   Italian parsley

Put the clams in a large heavy-based saucepan with 1 cup water. Cover and simmer for about 4 minutes, or until they open. Discard any that do not open.

Strain the liquid through a cheesecloth-lined sieve and reserve. Pull most of the clams out of their shells, leaving a few intact as a garnish.

Heat the oil in a saucepan. Add the bacon, onion, and garlic and cook, stirring, over medium heat until the onion is soft and the bacon golden. Add the potato and stir well.

Add enough water to the reserved clam liquid to make 1⅓ cups of liquid in total. Pour this and the stock into the saucepan and bring to a boil. Pour in the milk and bring back to a boil. Reduce the heat, cover and simmer for 20 minutes, or until the potato is tender.

Uncover and simmer for 10 minutes, or until slightly thickened. Add the cream, clam meat, and parsley and season. Heat through gently, but do not allow to boil. Serve with the clams in shells as a garnish.

SERVES 4

Jerusalem artichoke
and roast garlic soup

1 garlic head
1½ oz butter
1 tablespoon olive oil
1 onion, chopped
1 leek, white part only, chopped
1 celery stalk, chopped
1 lb 9 oz Jerusalem artichokes, peeled and chopped
1 small potato, chopped
6 cups vegetable or chicken stock
olive oil, to serve
finely chopped chives, to garnish

Preheat the oven to 400°F. Slice the base from the head of garlic, wrap it in foil and roast for 30 minutes, or until soft. When cool enough to handle, remove from the foil and slip the cloves from the skin. Set aside.

Heat the butter and oil in a large heavy-based saucepan over medium heat. Add the onion, leek, and celery and a large pinch of salt and cook for 10 minutes, or until soft. Add the Jerusalem artichokes, potato, and garlic and cook for a further 10 minutes. Pour in the stock and bring the mixture to a boil. Reduce the heat and simmer for 30 minutes, or until the vegetables are soft. Allow to cool slightly.

Purée the mixture in a blender until smooth, and season well. Serve with a drizzle of olive oil and garnish with chives.

SERVES 4

Lobster soup with zucchini and avocado

1¾ oz butter
1 garlic clove, crushed
2 shallots, finely chopped
1 onion, chopped
1 zucchini, diced
2½ tablespoons dry white wine
1⅔ cups fish stock
9 oz raw chopped lobster meat
1 cup heavy whipping cream
1 avocado, diced

1 tablespoon chopped cilantro leaves
1 tablespoon chopped Italian parsley
lemon juice, to serve

Fish substitution
crayfish, shrimp

Melt the butter in a large saucepan over medium heat. Add the garlic, chopped shallots, onion, and zucchini and cook for 8–10 minutes, or until the vegetables are just soft.

Add the wine and bring to a boil, then simmer for 3 minutes. Pour in the stock and bring to a boil again. Reduce the heat to low, add the lobster and simmer for 3–4 minutes, or until the lobster meat is opaque and tinged pink. Gently stir in the cream and season well.

Ladle the soup into four bowls and stir some of the avocado, cilantro, and parsley into each one. Squeeze a little lemon juice over the soup before serving.

SERVES 4

spicy

Vegetable and lentil soup with spiced yogurt

2 tablespoons olive oil
1 leek, white part only, chopped
2 garlic cloves, crushed
2 teaspoons curry powder
1 teaspoon ground cumin
1 teaspoon garam masala
4 cups vegetable stock
1 bay leaf
1 cup brown lentils
½ small pumpkin, such as
  butternut, peeled and cut
  into ½-inch cubes
2 zucchini, cut in half
  lengthways and sliced

1¾ cups canned crushed
  tomatoes
3½ cups small broccoli florets
1 small carrot, diced
½ cup peas
1 tablespoon chopped mint

Spiced yogurt
1 cup plain yogurt
1 tablespoon chopped cilantro
  leaves
1 garlic clove, crushed
3 dashes Tabasco sauce

Heat the oil in a saucepan over medium heat. Add the leek and garlic and cook for 4 minutes. Add the curry powder, cumin, and garam masala and cook for 1 minute. Add the stock, bay leaf, lentils, and squash. Bring to a boil, then reduce the heat and simmer for 10–15 minutes, or until the lentils are tender. Season. Add the zucchini, tomato, broccoli, carrot, and 2 cups water and simmer for 10 minutes, or until the vegetables are tender. Add the peas and simmer for 2–3 minutes.

To make the spiced yogurt, put the yogurt, cilantro, garlic, and Tabasco in a bowl, and stir until combined. Serve with the soup and garnish with the mint.

SERVES 6

Spicy pumpkin
and coconut soup

1 small red chili, seeded and chopped
1 lemon grass stem, white part only, sliced
1 teaspoon ground coriander
1 tablespoon chopped fresh ginger
2 cups vegetable stock
2 tablespoons oil
1 onion, finely chopped
5⅓ cups cubed pumpkin, such as butternut
1½ cups coconut milk
3 tablespoons chopped cilantro leaves
2 teaspoons shaved palm sugar or brown sugar
extra cilantro leaves, to garnish

Put the chili, lemon grass, ground coriander, ginger, and 2 tablespoons of vegetable stock in a food processor and process until smooth.

Heat the oil in a large saucepan over medium heat. Add the onion and cook for 5 minutes. Add the spice paste and cook, stirring, for 1 minute.

Add the squash and remaining vegetable stock. Bring to a boil, then reduce the heat and simmer, covered, for 15–20 minutes, or until the squash is tender. Cool slightly, then process in a food processor or blender until smooth. Return to the pan, stir in the coconut milk, cilantro, and palm sugar and simmer until hot. Garnish with the extra cilantro leaves.

SERVES 4

Tunisian fish soup

3 tablespoons olive oil
1 onion, chopped
1 celery stalk, chopped
4 garlic cloves, crushed
2 tablespoons tomato paste
1½ teaspoons ground turmeric
1½ teaspoons ground cumin
2 teaspoons harissa
4 cups fish stock
2 bay leaves
1 cup orzo or other small pasta

1 lb 2 oz mixed skinless snapper
    and sea bass fillets, cut into
    bite-sized chunks
2 tablespoons chopped mint,
    plus extra leaves,
    to garnish
2 tablespoons lemon juice
pita bread rounds, to serve
    (optional)

Fish substitution
cod, haddock, ocean perch,
    coral trout

Heat the oil in a large saucepan over medium heat. Add the onion and celery and cook for 8–10 minutes, or until softened. Add the garlic and cook for a further minute. Stir in the tomato paste, turmeric, cumin, and harissa and cook, stirring constantly, for an extra 30 seconds.

Pour the fish stock into the saucepan and add the bay leaves. Bring the liquid to a boil, then reduce the heat to low and simmer gently for 15 minutes.

Add the orzo to the liquid and cook for 2–3 minutes, or until *al dente*. Add the fish to the liquid and poach gently for 3–4 minutes, or until the fish is opaque. Stir in the mint and lemon juice and season to taste. Serve with warm pita bread, if desired. Garnish with mint leaves.

SERVES 6

Japanese shrimp,
scallop, and noodle soup

4 dried shiitake mushrooms
3½ oz dried soba or somen
  noodles
¼ oz sachet bonito-flavored
  soup stock (bouillon)
1 small carrot, cut into thin
  batons
¾ cup cubed firm tofu
16 shrimp, peeled and deveined,
  with tails intact
8 scallops, cleaned

2 scallions, finely chopped
1 tablespoon mirin
shichimi togarashi, to serve
  (see Note)

Fish substitution
chunks of firm white fish,
  fish balls

Soak the mushrooms in 1¼ cups boiling water for 30 minutes. Cook the noodles in a saucepan of boiling water for 2 minutes, then drain and rinse with cold water. Return the noodles to the pan and cover.

In a saucepan, mix the stock with 4 cups water. Drain the mushrooms and add the soaking liquid to the pan. Chop the mushroom caps. Add the mushrooms and carrot to the pan and bring to a boil. Reduce the heat to a simmer and cook for 5 minutes. Add the tofu, shrimp, scallops, scallion, and mirin. Simmer for 4 minutes, or until the shrimp are pink.

Meanwhile, pour hot water over the noodles. Drain. Divide the noodles among four large bowls and pour the soup over, dividing the seafood equally. Serve sprinkled with shichimi togarashi.

SERVES 4

NOTE: Shichimi togarashi is a Japanese condiment.

Split pea and vegetable soup

1 tablespoon peanut or vegetable oil
1 onion, chopped
2 garlic cloves, chopped
1½ teaspoons chopped fresh ginger
1½ tablespoons Madras curry paste
½ cup yellow split peas, rinsed and drained
1 large zucchini, peeled and chopped
1 large carrot, roughly chopped
2½ cups roughly chopped button mushrooms
1 celery stalk, roughly chopped
4 cups vegetable stock
½ cup light whipping cream
naan bread, to serve (optional)

Heat the oil in a saucepan, add the onion and cook over low heat for 5 minutes, or until soft. Add the garlic, ginger, and curry paste and cook over medium heat for 2 minutes. Stir in the split peas until well coated with paste, then add the zucchini, carrot, mushroom, and celery and cook for 2 minutes.

Add the stock, bring to a boil, then reduce the heat and simmer, partly covered, for 1 hour. Remove from the heat and allow to cool slightly.

Transfer the soup to a blender or food processor and process in batches until smooth. Return to the pan, stir in the cream and gently heat until warmed through. Serve with naan bread, if desired.

SERVES 4

Moroccan lamb, chickpea and cilantro soup

¾ cup dried chickpeas
1 tablespoon olive oil
1 lb 14 oz boned lamb leg, cut into ½-inch cubes
1 onion, chopped
2 garlic cloves, crushed
½ teaspoon ground cinnamon
½ teaspoon ground turmeric
½ teaspoon ground ginger
4 tablespoons chopped cilantro leaves
3½ cups canned crushed tomatoes
4 cups chicken stock
⅔ cup dried red lentils, rinsed
cilantro leaves, to garnish

Soak the chickpeas in cold water overnight. Drain and rinse well.

Heat the oil in a large saucepan over high heat and brown the lamb in batches for 2–3 minutes. Reduce the heat to medium, return the lamb to the pan with the onion and garlic and cook for 5 minutes. Add the spices, season and cook for 2 minutes. Add the cilantro, tomato, stock, and 2 cups water and bring to a boil over high heat.

Add the lentils and chickpeas and simmer, covered, over low heat for 1½ hours. Uncover and cook for 30 minutes, or until the lamb is tender and the soup is thick. Season. Garnish with cilantro.

SERVES 4–6

Saffron and Jerusalem artichoke soup

1 pinch of saffron threads
9 oz Jerusalem artichokes
2 tablespoons lemon juice
1 tablespoon olive oil
1 large onion, finely chopped
4 cups vegetable or chicken stock
3 teaspoons ground cumin
3 all-purpose potatoes, grated
2 teaspoons lemon juice, extra

Put the saffron threads in a bowl with 2 tablespoons boiling water and set aside.

Peel and thinly slice the artichokes, dropping the slices into a bowl of water mixed with lemon juice to prevent discoloration.

Heat the oil in a large heavy-based saucepan over medium heat. Add the onion and cook for 2–3 minutes, or until the onion is softened. Bring the stock to a boil in a large saucepan. Add the cumin to the onion mixture and cook for a further 30 seconds, or until fragrant. Add the drained artichokes, potato, saffron mixture, stock, and extra lemon juice. Bring to a boil, then reduce the heat and simmer for 15–18 minutes, or until the artichokes are very soft.

Transfer to a blender and process in batches until smooth. Return the soup to the pan and season to taste. Reheat over medium heat and serve immediately.

SERVES 4

Cold spicy roast pepper soup

4 red peppers
2 teaspoons oil
2 garlic cloves, crushed
4 scallions, sliced
1 teaspoon finely chopped seeded chilies
1¾ cups canned crushed tomatoes
½ cup chilled vegetable stock
1 teaspoon balsamic vinegar
2 tablespoons chopped basil

Cut the peppers into quarters and remove the seeds and membrane. Put the peppers, skin side up, under a hot broiler and broil until the skins blacken and blister. Cool in a plastic bag, then peel away the skin and roughly chop the flesh.

Heat the oil in a small saucepan. Add the garlic, scallion, and chili and cook over low heat for 1–2 minutes, or until softened.

Transfer to a food processor or blender, and add the pepper, crushed tomatoes, and stock. Blend until smooth, then stir in the vinegar and basil. Season to taste. Refrigerate, then serve cold.

SERVES 4

Carrot and ginger soup

3 cups vegetable stock
1 tablespoon oil
1 onion, chopped
1 tablespoon grated fresh ginger
8 carrots, chopped
2 tablespoons chopped cilantro leaves

Put the stock in a saucepan and bring to a boil.

Heat the oil in a large heavy-based saucepan over medium heat. Add the onion and ginger and cook for 2 minutes, or until the onion has softened.

Add the stock and carrots. Bring to a boil, then reduce the heat and simmer for 10–15 minutes, or until the carrot is cooked and tender.

Pour into a blender or food processor and process in batches until smooth. Return to the pan and add a little more stock or water if needed.

Stir in the cilantro and season to taste. Heat gently before serving.

SERVES 4

Pork congee

1½ cups long-grain rice, thoroughly rinsed
½ star anise
2 scallions, white part only
1½- x 1½-inch piece fresh ginger, cut into slices
14 cups chicken stock
1 tablespoon peanut oil
2 garlic cloves, crushed
1 teaspoon grated ginger, extra

14 oz ground pork
ground white pepper
3 tablespoons light soy sauce
sesame oil, to drizzle
6 fried dough sticks (optional, see Note)

Put the rice in a large saucepan with the star anise, scallions, sliced ginger, and chicken stock. Bring to a boil, then reduce the heat to low and simmer for 1½ hours, stirring occasionally.

Heat the oil in a frying pan over high heat. Cook the garlic and grated ginger for 30 seconds. Add the pork and cook for 5 minutes, or until browned, breaking up any lumps with a spoon.

Remove the star anise, scallions, and ginger from the soup and discard. Add the pork mixture and simmer for 10 minutes. Season with white pepper and stir in the soy sauce. Serve with a drizzle of sesame oil and fried dough sticks, if desired.

SERVES 4–6

NOTE: Fried dough sticks are available at Chinese bakeries and specialty shops and are best eaten soon after purchasing. If not, reheat in a 400°F oven for 5 minutes, then serve.

Soba noodle and vegetable soup

9 oz soba noodles
2 dried shiitake mushrooms
8 cups vegetable stock
1½ cups snow peas, cut into strips
2 small carrots, cut into thin 2-inch strips
2 garlic cloves, finely chopped
6 scallions, cut into 2-inch lengths
   and thinly sliced lengthways
1¼-inch piece fresh ginger, cut into julienne strips
4 tablespoons soy sauce
3 tablespoons mirin or sake
1 cup trimmed bean sprouts
cilantro leaves, to garnish

Cook the noodles according to the packet instructions. Drain.

Soak the mushrooms in ½ cup boiling water until soft. Drain, reserving the liquid. Remove the stalks and slice the mushrooms.

Combine the stock, mushrooms, reserved liquid, snow peas, carrot, garlic, scallion, and ginger in a large saucepan. Bring slowly to a boil, then reduce the heat to low and simmer for 5 minutes, or until the vegetables are tender. Add the soy sauce, mirin, and bean sprouts. Cook for a further 3 minutes.

Divide the noodles among four large serving bowls. Ladle the hot liquid and vegetables over the top and garnish with cilantro.

SERVES 4

Spicy tomato soup
with chorizo

1 lb 2 oz chorizo sausage
2 tablespoons olive oil
3 onions, halved and sliced
3 garlic cloves, thinly sliced
½ teaspoon ground cumin
1 teaspoon paprika
1–2 small red chilies, seeded and finely chopped
6 cups chicken stock
3½ cups canned crushed tomatoes
4 tablespoons chopped Italian parsley

Fill a large deep frying pan with about 1¼ inches cold water. Add the chorizo sausage, then bring to the boil over high heat. Reduce the heat and simmer, turning occasionally, for 15 minutes, or until the water evaporates, then continue to cook in any fat left in the pan for 3–4 minutes, or until the chorizo is lightly browned. Allow to cool slightly and break into bite-sized pieces.

Heat the oil in a large saucepan over medium heat. Cook the onion and garlic for 5–6 minutes, or until soft. Stir in the cumin, paprika, chili, chicken stock, tomato, and half the parsley. Bring to a boil and add the chorizo. Reduce the heat and simmer for 20 minutes. Stir in the remaining parsley and serve immediately.

SERVES 4–6

Duck, mushrooms, and rice noodle broth

3 dried shiitake mushrooms
1 Chinese roast duck (3 lbs 5 oz)
2 cups chicken stock
2 tablespoons light soy sauce
1 tablespoon Chinese rice wine
2 teaspoons sugar
14 oz fresh flat rice noodles
2 tablespoons oil
3 scallions, thinly sliced

1 teaspoon finely chopped fresh
  ginger
14 oz bok choy (pak choy),
  trimmed and leaves
  separated
¼ teaspoon sesame oil

Place the shiitake mushrooms in a bowl, cover with 1 cup boiling water and soak for 20 minutes. Drain, reserving the liquid and squeezing the excess liquid from the mushrooms. Discard the woody stems and slice the caps.

Remove the skin and flesh from the roast duck. Discard the fat and carcass. Finely slice the duck meat and the skin.

Place the chicken stock, soy sauce, rice wine, sugar, and the reserved mushroom liquid in a saucepan over medium heat. Bring to a simmer and cook for 5 minutes.

Meanwhile, place the rice noodles in a heatproof bowl, cover with boiling water and soak. Gently separate the noodles and drain. Divide among soup bowls.

Heat the oil in a wok over high heat. Add the scallion, ginger, and shiitake mushrooms and cook for several seconds. Transfer to the broth with the bok choy and duck meat and simmer for 1 minute, or until the duck has warmed through. Ladle the soup over the noodles and drizzle sesame oil on each serving.

SERVES 4–6

Spicy Portuguese
chicken soup

10 cups chicken stock
1 onion, cut into thin wedges
1 celery stalk, finely chopped
1 teaspoon grated lemon zest
3 firm, ripe tomatoes, peeled, seeded, and chopped
1 mint sprig
1 tablespoon olive oil
2 boneless, skinless chicken breasts
1 cup long-grain rice
2 tablespoons lemon juice
2 tablespoons shredded mint

Combine the chicken stock, onion, celery, lemon zest, tomato, mint, and olive oil in a large saucepan. Slowly bring to a boil, then reduce the heat, add the chicken and simmer gently for 20–25 minutes, or until the chicken is cooked through.

Remove the chicken from the saucepan and discard the mint sprig. Allow the chicken to cool, then thinly slice.

Meanwhile, add the rice to the pan and simmer for 25–30 minutes, or until the rice is tender. Return the sliced chicken to the pan, add the lemon juice and stir for 1–2 minutes, or until the chicken is warmed through. Season and stir through the mint.

SERVES 6

Spicy parsnip soup

5 cups vegetable or chicken stock
1 oz butter
1 white onion, cut into quarters and finely sliced
1 leek, white part only, finely sliced
1 lb 2 oz parsnips, peeled and finely sliced
1 tablespoon Madras curry powder
1 teaspoon ground cumin
1¼ cups light whipping cream (see Note)
⅓ cup cilantro leaves

Bring the stock to a boil in a saucepan and keep at a low simmer.

Melt the butter in a large saucepan over medium heat. Add the onion, leek, and parsnip and cook, covered, for 5 minutes. Add the curry powder and cumin and cook for 1 minute. Stir in the stock and cook, covered, over medium heat for about 10 minutes, or until tender.

Transfer the soup to a blender or food processor and blend in batches until smooth. Return to the pan. Stir in the cream and warm through over low heat. Season to taste and scatter with cilantro leaves.

SERVES 6

NOTE: This soup is also delicious without the cream, if you prefer not to add it.

Spicy seafood and roasted corn soup

2 sweet ears of corn
1 tablespoon olive oil
1 red onion, finely chopped
1 small red chili, finely chopped
½ teaspoon ground allspice
4 vine-ripened tomatoes, peeled and finely diced
6 cups fish stock or light chicken stock
10½ oz boneless firm white fish fillets, diced

7 oz fresh crab meat
7 oz peeled raw shrimp, roughly chopped
1 tablespoon lime juice

Quesadillas
4 flour tortillas (7½ inch)
⅔ cup grated cheddar cheese
1 large handful cilantro leaves
2 tablespoons olive oil

Preheat the oven to 400°F. Peel back the husks on the ears of corn and remove the silks. Fold the husks back over the corn, put in a baking dish and bake for 1 hour, or until the corn is tender.

Heat the oil in a saucepan over medium heat. Add the onion and cook until soft. Add the chili and allspice and cook for 1 minute, then add the tomato and stock and bring to a boil. Reduce the heat and simmer, covered, for 45 minutes. Slice the kernels from the ears of corn, add to the soup and simmer for 15 minutes. Add the fish, crab, and shrimp meat and simmer for 5 minutes. Add the lime juice.

Meanwhile, to make the quesadillas, top one tortilla with half the cheese and half the cilantro. Season, then top with another tortilla. Heat 1 tablespoon of the oil in a frying pan and cook the quesadilla for 30 seconds on each side. Repeat. Cut into wedges and serve with the soup.

SERVES 4

Five-spice duck and somen noodle soup

4 duck breasts, skin on
1 teaspoon Chinese five-spice
1 teaspoon peanut oil
7 oz dried somen noodles

Star anise broth
4 cups chicken stock
3 star anise
5 scallions, chopped
1 large handful cilantro leaves, chopped

Preheat the oven to 400°F. Trim the duck breast of excess fat, then lightly sprinkle both sides with the five-spice powder.

Heat the oil in a large frying pan over medium heat. Add the duck, skin side down, and cook for 2–3 minutes, or until brown and crisp. Turn and cook the other side for 3 minutes. Transfer to a roasting tray and cook, skin side up, for a further 8–10 minutes, or until cooked to your liking.

Meanwhile, put the chicken stock and star anise in a small saucepan. Bring to a boil, then reduce the heat and simmer for 5 minutes. Add the scallion and cilantro and simmer for 5 minutes.

Cook the noodles in a saucepan of boiling water for 2 minutes, or until soft. Drain and divide among four bowls. Ladle the broth over the noodles and top each bowl with one sliced duck breast.

SERVES 4

Chickpea, potato, and spinach soup

4 cups vegetable stock
1½ tablespoons olive oil
1 onion, finely chopped
1 large potato, cut into ½-inch cubes
1½ teaspoons paprika
2 garlic cloves, crushed
1¾ cups canned chickpeas, drained
1 large firm, ripe tomato, cut into small cubes
1 cup coarsely shredded spinach
¼ cup grated parmesan cheese

Put the stock in a saucepan, then cover and slowly bring to a boil.

Heat the olive oil in a large heavy-based saucepan. Cook the onion for 2 minutes, or until soft. Add the potato to the onion, and stir in the paprika, garlic, and chickpeas. Add the onion mixture to the stock and bring to a boil. Stir in the tomato and season.

Simmer for 10 minutes, or until the potato is tender. Add the spinach and cook until wilted. Top with parmesan and season to taste.

SERVES 4

hearty

Pepper, spinach, and chickpea soup

1 tablespoon olive oil
8 scallions, finely sliced
1 red pepper
1 garlic clove, crushed
1 teaspoon cumin seeds
1½ cups tomato purée
3 cups vegetable or beef stock
2 cups canned chickpeas, rinsed and drained
2 teaspoons red wine vinegar
1–2 teaspoons sugar
2¼ cups baby spinach leaves

Heat the oil in a large heavy-based saucepan over medium heat and stir in the scallion. Reduce the heat and cook, covered, for 2–3 minutes, or until softened.

Remove the seeds and membrane from the pepper and finely dice. Add the pepper, garlic, and cumin seeds to the pan and cook for 1 minute.

Add the tomato purée and stock and bring the mixture to a boil. Reduce the heat and simmer for 10 minutes. Add the chickpeas, vinegar, and sugar to the soup and simmer for a further 5 minutes. Stir in the baby spinach and season to taste. Cook until the spinach begins to wilt. Serve immediately.

SERVES 4

Chicken and
spinach risoni soup

1 tablespoon olive oil
1 leek, white part only, quartered lengthways and thinly sliced
2 garlic cloves, crushed
1 teaspoon ground cumin
6 cups chicken stock
2 boneless, skinless chicken breasts
1 cup risoni
3⅓ cups roughly chopped baby spinach leaves
1 tablespoon chopped dill
2 teaspoons lemon juice

Heat the oil in a large saucepan over low heat. Add the leek and cook for about 8–10 minutes, or until soft. Add the garlic and cumin and cook for 1 minute. Pour the stock into the pan, increase the heat to high and bring to a boil. Reduce the heat to low, add the chicken breasts and simmer, covered, for 8 minutes. Remove the chicken from the broth, allow to cool slightly, then shred.

Stir the risoni into the broth and simmer for 12 minutes, or until *al dente*.

Return the chicken to the broth along with the spinach and dill. Simmer for 2 minutes, or until the spinach has wilted. Stir in the lemon juice and season to taste.

SERVES 4

Pasta and bean soup

1 cup dried cranberry beans
3 tablespoons olive oil
3¼ oz pancetta or bacon, finely
   diced
1 onion, finely chopped
2 garlic cloves, crushed
1 celery stalk, thinly sliced
1 carrot, diced
1 bay leaf
1 rosemary sprig
1 Italian parsley sprig

1¾ cups canned crushed
   tomatoes, drained
6½ cups vegetable stock
2 tablespoons finely chopped
   Italian parsley
1 cup ditalini or other small
   dried pasta
extra virgin olive oil, to drizzle
freshly grated parmesan cheese,
   to serve

Put the cranberry beans in a large bowl, cover with cold water and leave to soak overnight. Drain and rinse.

Heat the oil in a large saucepan over medium heat. Add the pancetta, onion, garlic, celery, and carrot and cook for 5 minutes, or until golden. Season with black pepper. Add the bay leaf, rosemary, parsley, tomato, stock, and beans and bring to a boil. Reduce the heat and simmer for 1½ hours, or until the beans are tender. Add more boiling water if necessary to maintain the liquid level.

Discard the bay leaf, rosemary, and parsley sprigs. Scoop out 1 cup of the bean mixture and purée in a food processor or blender. Return to the pan, season and add the parsley and pasta. Simmer for 6 minutes, or until the pasta is *al dente*. Remove from the heat and set aside for 10 minutes. Serve drizzled with extra virgin olive oil and sprinkled with parmesan.

SERVES 4

Broth with ravioli

6 cups vegetable or chicken stock
1 lb 2 oz spinach and ricotta ravioli
2½ cups snow peas, sliced on the diagonal
4 tablespoons chopped Italian parsley
4 tablespoons chopped basil
grated parmesan cheese, to garnish

Place the stock in a large heavy-based saucepan and bring to a boil. Add the ravioli and cook for 8–10 minutes, or until the pasta is *al dente*.

Season to taste and stir in the snow peas, parsley, and basil. Sprinkle with grated parmesan just before serving.

SERVES 2

Manhattan-style
seafood chowder

2¼ oz butter

3 bacon slices, chopped

2 onions, chopped

2 garlic cloves, finely chopped

2 celery stalks, sliced

3 potatoes, diced

3 teaspoons chopped thyme

5 cups fish stock

2 lbs 4 oz baby clams

1 tablespoon tomato paste

1¾ cups canned crushed
   tomatoes

13 oz skinless ling fillets, cut
   into bite-sized pieces

12 large shrimp, peeled and
   deveined, with tails intact

2 tablespoons chopped Italian
   parsley

Fish substitution

cod, flake, hake

Melt the butter in a saucepan over low heat. Add the bacon, onion, garlic, and celery and cook, stirring occasionally, for 5 minutes, or until soft. Add the potato, thyme, and 4 cups of the stock to the saucepan and bring to a boil. Reduce the heat and simmer, covered, for 15 minutes. Pour the remaining stock into a saucepan and bring to a boil. Add the clams, cover and cook for 3–5 minutes, or until they open. Discard any that do not open. Drain the clam liquid through a cheesecloth-lined sieve and add to the soup mixture. Pull most of the clams out of their shells, leaving a few intact to garnish.

Stir the tomato paste and crushed tomatoes into the soup and bring back to a boil. Add the fish, clams, and shrimp and simmer over low heat for 3 minutes, or until the seafood is cooked. Season and stir in the parsley. Serve garnished with the clams in their shells.

SERVES 4

Mushroom and tortellini soup

1 tablespoon olive oil
2 cups small flat mushrooms, sliced
6 scallions, sliced
1 small garlic clove, crushed
5 cups vegetable or chicken stock
1 tablespoon port
2 teaspoons worcestershire sauce
7 oz fresh large ricotta tortellini
shaved parmesan cheese, to garnish

Heat the oil in a large heavy-based saucepan over high heat. Add the mushrooms and cook for 2 minutes, browning the mushrooms before turning. Add the scallion and garlic and cook for a further 1 minute.

Meanwhile, bring the stock to a boil in a separate saucepan. Add the stock, port, and worcestershire sauce to the mushroom mixture and bring to a boil. Add the tortellini and simmer for 8 minutes, or until the tortellini is *al dente*.

Season to taste and serve topped with shaved parmesan.

SERVES 4

Seafood soup with rouille

Rouille

1 cooked floury potato, peeled and diced

1 red pepper, broiled and peeled

2 garlic cloves, chopped

1 egg yolk

½ cup olive oil

4 cups fish stock

½ teaspoon saffron threads

4 thyme sprigs

2-inch piece orange zest

1 small baguette

olive oil, for brushing

10½ oz salmon fillet, cut into 4 pieces

10½ oz ling fillet, cut into 4 pieces

1 squid tube, cleaned and cut into rings

8 raw large shrimp, peeled and deveined

To make the rouille, place the potato, pepper, garlic, and egg yolk in a food processor and process until smooth. With the motor running, gradually add the olive oil until the mixture has the consistency of mayonnaise.

Preheat the oven to 350°F. Put the stock in a large saucepan and bring to a boil. Add the saffron, thyme, and orange zest. Remove from the heat and leave to stand for 10 minutes to allow the flavors to infuse.

Meanwhile, cut the baguette into ½-inch thick slices. Brush with oil and put on a baking tray. Bake for 10 minutes, or until crisp and golden.

Strain the stock and return to a boil, then add the salmon, ling, squid rings, and shrimp. Remove the stock from the heat and leave for 2 minutes, or until the seafood is cooked. Serve with the rouille and croutons.

SERVES 4

Zuppa di faggioli

4½ cups canned cannellini
   beans
1 tablespoon extra virgin olive oil
1 leek, white part only, finely
   chopped
2 garlic cloves, crushed
1 teaspoon thyme leaves
2 celery stalks, diced
1 carrot, diced
10 Swiss chard stalks, trimmed
   and roughly chopped

1 firm, ripe tomato, diced
4 cups vegetable stock
2 small crusty rolls, each cut into
   4 slices
2 teaspoons balsamic vinegar
⅓ cup finely grated parmesan
   cheese

Put half of the cannellini beans and half of the liquid in a blender or food processor and blend until smooth. Drain the remaining beans and set aside.

Heat the oil in a large heavy-based saucepan over medium heat. Add the leek, garlic, and thyme and cook for 2–3 minutes, or until soft and aromatic. Add the celery, carrot, Swiss chard, and tomato and cook for a further 2–3 minutes, or until the chard has wilted. Heat the stock in a separate saucepan.

Stir the puréed cannellini beans and stock into the vegetable mixture. Bring to a boil, then reduce the heat and simmer for 5–10 minutes, or until the vegetables are tender. Add the drained beans and stir until heated through. Season to taste.

Arrange 2 slices of bread in the base of each soup bowl. Stir the balsamic vinegar into the soup and ladle over the bread. Serve topped with grated parmesan.

SERVES 4

Chunky fish soup with bacon and dumplings

2 tablespoons olive oil
1 onion, chopped
1 small red pepper, chopped
1 small zucchini, diced
5½ oz smoked bacon, chopped
1 garlic clove, crushed
2 tablespoons paprika
1¾ cups canned crushed
    tomatoes
2½ cups canned chickpeas
1 lb skinless pike fillet, cut into
    large pieces

2 tablespoons chopped
    Italian parsley

Dumplings
½ cup self-rising flour
1 egg, lightly beaten
1½ tablespoons whole milk
2 teaspoons finely chopped
    marjoram

Fish substitution
bream, char, trout

Heat the oil in a saucepan over low heat. Add the onion and cook for 8 minutes, or until softened. Add the pepper, zucchini, bacon, and garlic and cook over medium heat for 5 minutes, stirring occasionally.

Meanwhile, to make the dumplings, combine the flour, egg, milk, and marjoram in a bowl and mix with a wooden spoon.

Add the paprika, tomato, chickpeas, and 3¼ cups water to the vegetables. Bring the liquid to a boil, then reduce the heat to low and simmer for 10 minutes, or until thickened slightly. Using two tablespoons to help you form the dumplings, add six rounds of the dumpling mixture to the soup. Poach for about 2 minutes, then slide the pieces of fish into the liquid. Poach for a further 2–3 minutes, or until the fish is cooked. Season to taste and sprinkle with parsley.

SERVES 6

Minestrone alla Milanese

1¼ cups dried cranberry beans
2 oz butter
1 onion, finely chopped
1 garlic clove, finely chopped
3 tablespoons Italian parsley, finely chopped
2 sage leaves
3½ oz pancetta, cubed
2 celery stalks, halved, then sliced
2 carrots, sliced
3 potatoes, peeled but left whole
1 teaspoon tomato paste

1¾ cups canned crushed tomatoes
8 basil leaves
12 cups chicken or vegetable stock
2 zucchini, sliced
1⅓ cups shelled peas
1 cup green beans, cut into 1½-inch lengths
¼ cabbage, shredded
1 cup risotto rice
grated parmesan cheese, to serve

Put the dried beans in a large bowl, cover with cold water and soak overnight. Drain and rinse under cold water.

Melt the butter in a saucepan and add the onion, garlic, parsley, sage, and pancetta. Cook over low heat, stirring until the onion is soft.

Add the celery, carrot, and potatoes, and cook for 5 minutes. Stir in the tomato paste, tomato, basil, and cranberry beans. Season with pepper. Add the stock and bring slowly to a boil. Cover and leave to simmer for 2 hours, stirring once or twice.

If the potatoes have not broken up, roughly break them with a fork. Season to taste and add the zucchini, peas, green beans, cabbage, and rice. Simmer until the rice is cooked. Serve with the parmesan cheese.

SERVES 6

Goulash soup with dumplings

3 tablespoons olive oil
2 lbs 4 oz chuck steak, cut into
    ½-inch cubes
2 large onions, chopped
3 garlic cloves, crushed
1 green pepper, chopped
1½ teaspoons caraway seeds,
    ground
3 tablespoons sweet paprika
¼ teaspoon ground nutmeg
pinch cayenne pepper
½ teaspoon sea salt
1¾ cups canned crushed
    tomatoes

8 cups chicken stock
2 potatoes, diced
1 green pepper, julienned
2 tablespoons sour cream

Dumplings

1 egg
3 tablespoons finely grated
    parmesan cheese
⅔ cup self-rising flour
pinch cayenne pepper

Heat half the oil in a saucepan over medium heat. Cook the beef in batches for
1–2 minutes. Remove and set aside. Heat the remaining oil in the pan over low heat.
Add the onion, garlic, and chopped pepper and cook for 5–6 minutes, or until
softened. Stir in the spices and salt. Return the beef to the pan. Stir in the tomato
and stock and bring to a boil. Reduce the heat to low and simmer, covered, for
1¼ hours. Add the potato and cook for 30 minutes. Stir in the julienned pepper and
sour cream.

To make the dumplings, combine the ingredients and a pinch of salt to form a
dough. Turn onto a floured surface and knead for 5 minutes. Roll ½ teaspoonfuls
of the dough into balls, drop into the soup and cook for 6 minutes.

SERVES 4–6

Spaghetti and meatball soup

5½ oz spaghetti, broken into
   3-inch lengths
6 cups beef stock
3 teaspoons tomato paste
1¾ cups canned crushed
   tomatoes
3 tablespoons torn basil leaves
shaved parmesan cheese,
   to garnish

Meatballs
1 tablespoon oil
1 onion, finely chopped
2 garlic cloves, crushed
1 lb 2 oz lean ground beef
3 tablespoons finely chopped
   Italian parsley
3 tablespoons fresh breadcrumbs
2 tablespoons finely grated
   parmesan cheese
1 egg, lightly beaten

Cook the spaghetti in a large saucepan of boiling water according to packet instructions until *al dente*. Drain. Put the stock and 2 cups water in a large saucepan and slowly bring to a simmer.

Meanwhile, to make the meatballs, heat the oil in a frying pan over medium heat. Cook the onion for 2 minutes, or until soft. Add the garlic. Cook for 30 seconds. Allow to cool. Combine the beef, parsley, breadcrumbs, parmesan, egg, the onion mixture, and season. Roll heaped teaspoons of mixture into balls, making 40 balls.

Stir the tomato paste and tomato into the beef stock and simmer for 2–3 minutes. Drop in the meatballs, return to a simmer and cook for 10 minutes, or until cooked through. Stir in the spaghetti and basil to warm through. Season and top with shaved parmesan.

SERVES 4

Winter lamb shank soup

1 tablespoon olive oil
2 lbs 12 oz lamb shanks
2 onions, chopped
4 garlic cloves, chopped
1 cup red wine
2 bay leaves
1 tablespoon chopped rosemary
10 cups beef stock
1¾ cups canned crushed
   tomatoes

¾ cup pearl barley, rinsed and
   drained
1 large carrot, diced
1 potato, diced
1 turnip, diced
1 parsnip, diced
2 tablespoons redcurrant jelly
   (optional)

Heat the oil in a saucepan over high heat. Cook the lamb shanks for 2–3 minutes, or until brown. Remove from the pan.

Add the onion to the pan and cook over low heat for 8 minutes, or until soft. Add the garlic and cook for 30 seconds, then add the wine and simmer for 5 minutes.

Add the shanks, bay leaves, half the rosemary, and 6 cups of the stock to the pan. Season. Bring to a boil over high heat. Reduce the heat and simmer, covered, for 2 hours, or until the meat falls off the bone. Remove the shanks and cool slightly.

Remove the meat off the bone and roughly chop. Add to the broth with the tomato, barley, the remaining rosemary, and stock and simmer for 30 minutes. Add the vegetables and cook for 1 hour, or until the barley is tender. Remove the bay leaves, then stir in the redcurrant jelly.

SERVES 4

Swiss chard and risoni soup with gruyère croutons

1 oz butter
1 large onion, finely chopped
1 garlic clove, crushed
8 cups vegetable or chicken stock
1 cup risoni
½ baguette, cut into 6 slices
½ oz butter, extra, melted
1 teaspoon dijon mustard
½ cup coarsely grated gruyère cheese
4 Swiss chard stalks, shredded
½ cup torn basil

Heat the butter in a large heavy-based saucepan over medium heat. Add the onion and garlic and cook for 2–3 minutes, or until the onion is softened.

Meanwhile, put the stock in a large saucepan and bring to a boil. Add the stock to the onion mixture and bring to a boil. Add the risoni, reduce the heat and simmer for 8 minutes, stirring occasionally.

Meanwhile, put the baguette slices in a single layer on a baking sheet and cook under a preheated broiler until golden brown on one side. Turn the slices over and brush with the combined melted butter and mustard. Top with the gruyère and broil until the cheese has melted.

Add the Swiss chard and basil to the risoni mixture and simmer for about 1 minute, or until the risoni is *al dente*. Season and serve with the gruyère croutons.

SERVES 6

Tomato and pasta soup

5 cups vegetable or chicken stock
1 cup spiral pasta
2 carrots, sliced
1 zucchini, sliced
4 firm, ripe tomatoes, roughly chopped
2 tablespoons shredded basil

Place the stock in a heavy-based saucepan and bring to a boil. Reduce the heat, add the pasta, carrot, and zucchini and cook for about 5–10 minutes, or until the pasta is *al dente*.

Add the tomato and heat through gently for a few minutes. Season to taste.

Serve the soup sprinkled with the basil over the top.

SERVES 4

NOTE: To give this soup a slightly different flavor, serve with a dollop of fresh pesto.

Hearty seafood soup

2 tablespoons dried shrimp

3 tablespoons olive oil

1 large onion, finely chopped

3 garlic cloves, crushed

1 small red chili, deseeded and
finely chopped

1 teaspoon finely grated fresh
ginger

3 tablespoons crunchy peanut
butter

3½ cups canned crushed
tomatoes

1¾ oz creamed coconut,
chopped

1½ cups coconut milk

generous pinch of ground cloves

4 tablespoons chopped cilantro
leaves

1 lb 9 oz swordfish, cut into
large chunks

3½ oz small shrimp, peeled and
deveined

2 tablespoons chopped cashew
nuts

Fish substitution

marlin, tuna, monkfish

Soak the dried shrimp in boiling water for 10 minutes, then drain.

Heat the oil in a saucepan over medium heat. Cook the onion for 5 minutes. Add
the garlic, chili, and ginger and cook for 2 minutes. Stir in the drained dried shrimp,
peanut butter, tomato, creamed coconut, coconut milk, ground cloves, and half of
the cilantro. Bring the mixture to a boil and simmer gently for 10 minutes. Remove
from the heat, allow to cool slightly, then tip the sauce into a food processor or
blender and blend until thick and smooth.

Return the sauce to the pan over medium heat. Add the swordfish and cook for
2 minutes, then add the shrimp and continue to simmer until all the seafood is
cooked—the shrimp will be pink and the fish opaque. Serve with the cashews and
remaining cilantro sprinkled over the top.

SERVES 4

Tomato bread soup

6 firm, vine-ripened tomatoes
1 loaf day-old crusty Italian bread
1 tablespoon olive oil
3 garlic cloves, crushed
1 tablespoon tomato paste
5 cups hot vegetable stock
4 tablespoons torn basil leaves
2–3 tablespoons extra virgin olive oil
extra virgin olive oil, extra, to serve

Score a cross in the base of each tomato. Put in a bowl of boiling water for 1 minute, then plunge into cold water and peel the skin away from the cross. Cut the tomatoes in half and scoop out the seeds with a teaspoon. Chop the tomato flesh.

Remove most of the crust from the bread and discard. Cut the bread into 1¼-inch thick pieces.

Heat the oil in a large saucepan over medium heat. Add the garlic, tomato, and tomato paste, then reduce the heat and simmer, stirring occasionally, for about 10–15 minutes, or until reduced and thickened. Add the stock and bring to a boil, stirring for 2–3 minutes. Reduce the heat to medium, add the bread pieces and cook, stirring, for 5 minutes, or until the bread softens and absorbs most of the liquid. Add more stock or water if necessary.

Stir in the torn basil leaves and extra virgin olive oil, and leave for 5 minutes to allow the flavors to develop. Drizzle with a little extra virgin olive oil to serve.

SERVES 4

Beef meatball and white bean soup

1 lb 5 oz ground beef
2 garlic cloves, crushed
1 tablespoon finely chopped
    Italian parsley
large pinch ground cinnamon
large pinch freshly grated
    nutmeg
2 eggs, lightly beaten
6 cups beef stock

2 carrots, thinly sliced
4½ cups canned white beans,
    drained
½ savoy cabbage, finely
    shredded
grated parmesan cheese,
    to serve

Put the beef in a bowl with the garlic, parsley, cinnamon, nutmeg, and half of the egg. Mix to combine and season well. If the mixture is dry, add the rest of the egg —it needs to be sticky enough so that forming small meatballs is easy.

Roll the beef mixture into small meatballs—they should be small enough to scoop up on a spoon and eat in one mouthful.

Put the beef stock and the carrot in a saucepan and bring to a boil. Add the meatballs, one at a time, and reduce the heat. Simmer for 3 minutes. Add the beans and cabbage and cook for a further 4–5 minutes. Season to taste. Serve with grated parmesan.

SERVES 4

index

A

artichokes
   Jerusalem artichoke and
      roast garlic soup 116
   saffron and Jerusalem
      artichoke soup 134
asparagus soup 38

B

beans
   beef and chili bean soup
      79
   beef meatball and white
      bean soup 195
   minestrone alla
      milanese 179
   pasta and bean soup 164
beef
   beef and chili bean soup
      79
   beef meatball and white
      bean soup 195
   beef pho 59
   goulash soup with
      dumplings 180
   spaghetti and meatball
      soup 183
   Vietnamese beef soup 68

borscht 41
bouillabaisse 34
broth with ravioli 167

C

cabbage soup 45
Caribbean fish soup 55
carrot and ginger soup 138
cauliflower and almond
    soup with hot cheese
    rolls 103
chicken
   chicken and galangal
      soup 56
   chicken and spinach
      risoni soup 163
   chicken and pumpkin
      laksa 64
   chicken and vegetable
      soup 22
   chicken, mushroom,
      and Madeira soup 108
   creamy chicken and
      corn soup 99
   curried chicken noodle
      soup 52
   spicy Portuguese
      chicken soup 149

chickpeas
   chickpea, potato, and
      spinach soup 157
   Moroccan lamb,
      chickpea, and cilantro
      soup 133
   pepper, spinach, and
      chickpea soup 160
chili
   beef and chili bean soup
      79
   beef pho 59
   Caribbean fish soup
      55
   chicken and galangal
      soup 56
   chili, corn, and red
      pepper soup 84
   hot and sour shrimp
      soup 75
   sweet potato and chili
      soup 48
   Thai spicy sour soup 63
chowder
   Manhattan-style
      seafood 168
   New England clam
      115

potato and sweet corn 104

shrimp, potato, and corn 92

clams

creamy clam soup 111

New England clam chowder 115

cold soups

borscht 41

gazpacho 33

spicy roast pepper soup 137

corn

corn and lemon grass soup with crayfish 100

creamy chicken and corn soup 99

spicy seafood and roasted corn soup 153

crab bisque 18

cream of fennel and leek soup 107

curry

curried chicken noodle soup 52

curried lentil, carrot, and cashew soup 67

green curry vegetable soup 76

tom yum goong 83

D

duck

duck, mushrooms, and rice noodle broth 146

five-spice duck and somen noodle soup 154

rice noodle soup with duck 72

dumplings

chunky fish soup with bacon and dumplings 176

goulash soup with dumplings 180

F

five-spice duck and somen noodle soup 154

French onion soup 10

G

gazpacho 33

goulash soup with dumplings 180

green curry vegetable soup 76

gumbo 80

J

Japanese shrimp, scallop, and noodle soup 129

Jerusalem artichoke and roast garlic soup 116

L

laksa 51

lamb

Moroccan lamb, chickpea, and cilantro soup 133

winter lamb shank soup 184

leeks

cream of fennel and leek soup 107

leek and potato soup 25

lentils

curried lentil, carrot, and cashew soup 67

lentil and Swiss chard soup 13

pumpkin and red lentil soup 71

vegetable and lentil soup with spiced yogurt 122

lobster soup with zucchini and avocado 119

M

Manhattan-style seafood chowder 168

Mexican soup with salsa 60

minestrone 26

minestrone alla milanese 179

Moroccan lamb, chickpea, and cilantro soup 133

mushrooms

chicken, mushroom, and Madeira soup 108

duck, mushrooms, and rice noodle broth 146

fresh mushroom, shallot, and sour cream soup 95

mushroom and tortellini soup 171

mushroom soup 30

N

New England clam chowder 115

noodles

duck, mushrooms, and rice noodle broth 146

five-spice duck and somen noodle soup 154

rice noodle soup with duck 72

soba noodle and vegetable soup 142

O

onions
    caramelized onion and
      parsnip soup 29
    French onion soup 10
orange sweet potato
    soup 91

P

pasta
    broth with ravioli 167
    chicken and spinach
      risoni soup 163
    mushroom and tortellini
      soup 171
    pasta and bean soup
      164
    spaghetti and meatball
      soup 183
    Swiss chard and risoni
      soup with gruyère
      croutons 187
    tomato and pasta soup
      188
peas
    pea and ham soup 37
    split pea and vegetable
      soup 130
peppers
    cold spicy roast pepper
      soup 137
    pepper, spinach, and
      chickpea soup 160
pork congee 141
potatoes
    chickpea, potato, and
      spinach soup 157
    goulash soup with
      dumplings 180
    leek and potato soup
      25
    potato and sweet corn
      chowder 104

    shrimp, potato, and
      corn chowder 92
pumpkin
    chicken and pumpkin
      laksa 64
    spicy pumpkin and
      coconut soup 125
    pumpkin and red lentil
      soup 71
    pumpkin soup 14

R

rice
    minestrone alla
      milanese 179
    pork congee 141
    rice noodle soup with
      duck 72

S

saffron and Jerusalem
    artichoke soup 134
seafood
    bouillabaisse 34
    Caribbean fish soup 55
    chunky fish soup
      with bacon and
      dumplings 176
    corn and lemon grass
      soup with crayfish
      100
    crab bisque 18
    creamy clam soup 111
    gumbo 80
    hearty seafood soup 191
    hot and sour shrimp
      soup 75
    Japanese shrimp,
      scallop, and noodle
      soup 129
    lobster soup with
      zucchini and avocado
      119

    Manhattan-style
      seafood chowder
      168
    Mexican soup with
      salsa 60
    New England clam
      chowder 115
    seafood soup with
      rouille 172
    shrimp, potato, and
      corn chowder 92
    spicy seafood and
      roasted corn soup 153
    tom yum goong 83
    Tunisian fish soup 126
shrimp
    hot and sour shrimp
      soup 75
    Japanese shrimp,
      scallop, and noodle
      soup 129
    shrimp, potato, and
      corn chowder 92
soba noodle and vegetable
    soup 142
spaghetti and meatball
    soup 183
spicy soups
    cold spicy roast pepper
      soup 137
    Moroccan lamb,
      chickpea, and cilantro
      soup 133
    spicy parsnip soup 150
    spicy Portuguese
      chicken soup 149
    spicy seafood and
      roasted corn soup 153
    spicy pumpkin and
      coconut soup 125
    spicy tomato soup with
      chorizo 145
    Thai spicy sour soup 63

Tunisian fish soup 126
vegetable and lentil
 soup with spiced
 yogurt 122
spinach soup 21
split pea and vegetable
 soup 130
spring vegetable soup
 with basil pesto 17
sweet potatoes
 orange sweet potato
 soup 91
 sweet potato and chili
 soup 48
 sweet potato and pear
 soup 112
Swiss chard and risoni
 soup with gruyère
 croutons 187

T
Thai spicy sour soup 63
tom yum goong 83

tomatoes
 minestrone alla
 milanese 179
 spicy tomato soup with
 chorizo 145
 tomato and pasta soup
 188
 tomato bread soup 192
Tunisian fish soup 126

V
vegetables
 asparagus soup 38
 cabbage soup 45
 carrot and ginger soup
 138
 gazpacho 33
 green curry vegetable
 soup 76
 minestrone 26
 spinach soup 21
 split pea and vegetable
 soup 130

spring vegetable soup
 with basil pesto 17
vegetable and lentil
 soup with spiced
 yogurt 122
vegetable soup 42
watercress soup 96
zucchini pesto soup 88
Vietnamese beef soup 68

W
watercress soup 96
winter lamb shank soup
 184

Y
yogurt, spiced 122

Z
zucchini pesto soup 88
zuppa di faggioli 175

Chief Executive: Juliet Rogers
Publishing Director: Kay Scarlett

Design manager: Vivien Valk
Series editor: Jane Price
Project manager: Gordana Trifunovic
Design concept: Alex Frampton
Designer: Susanne Geppert
Production: Nikla Martin
Introduction text: Leanne Kitchen
Recipes developed by the Murdoch Books Test Kitchen

Barnes & Noble, Inc.
122 Fifth Avenue
New York, NY 10011

ISBN-13: 978-1-4351-0823-3
ISBN-10: 1-4351-0823-X

10 9 8 7 6 5 4 3 2 1

Printed by Sing Cheong Printing Co. Ltd in 2008. PRINTED IN HONG KONG.

IMPORTANT: Those who might be at risk from the effects of salmonella poisoning
(the elderly, pregnant women, young children and those suffering from immune
deficiency diseases) should consult their doctor with any concerns about eating raw eggs.

OVEN GUIDE: You may find cooking times vary depending on the oven you are using.
For fan-forced ovens, as a general rule, set the oven temperature to 35°F lower than
indicated in the recipe.